ISBN 978-1-324-08394-8

AF192476

From his subway drawings to his iconic radiant baby, Keith Haring is one of the most immediately recognizable artists of his generation. And from his graffitied street art to his snubbing of art world conventions and his activism during the AIDS epidemic, rebellion was a constant. This vibrant visual biography tells his story in twelve paintings that reflect his life and work: childhood, music, drugs, sex, protest—and beyond. *Rebellious* paints an energetic, visceral portrait of Haring's unconventional life and how his art shaped and reflected the world around him and still resonates today.

REBELLIOUS

CONTENTS

"The freedom to be different, the freedom to speak what you want, the freedom to not fit exactly into the groove that people expect you to be in, the freedom to rebel against wrong, etc., is more and more important in a society where things become more and more controlled and more and more programmed."

"I think the role of an artist in any society is to be an antagonist, but especially in a conservative society, or in a politically oppressive society, which is increasingly more what we're living in all the time."

"If you paint with that attitude—that there are no mistakes—then there won't be any. If a line drips, then it drips."

"I'm still a kid at heart. I mean, in my head, I'm still 15 years old."

—KEITH HARING

To all the young people
who feel insecure—just as Keith did

Excerpts from *Radiant: The Life and Line of Keith Haring* by Brad Gooch.
Copyright © 2024 by Brad Gooch. Used by permission of HarperCollins Publishers.

Extracts from *KEITH HARING: The Authorized Biography* by John Gruen.
Copyright © 1991 by John Gruen, used by permission of The Wylie Agency LLC.

Excerpt(s) from *KEITH HARING JOURNALS: (PENGUIN CLASSICS DELUXE EDITION)* by Keith Haring,
copyright © 1996, 2010 by The Keith Haring Foundation, Inc. Used by permission of Penguin Classics,
an imprint of Penguin Publishing Group, a division of Penguin Random House LLC. All rights reserved.

For information about permission to reproduce selections from this book, write to
Permissions, W. W. Norton & Company, Inc., 500 Fifth Avenue, New York, NY 10110

For information about special discounts for bulk purchases, please contact
W. W. Norton Special Sales at specialsales@wwnorton.com or 800-233-4830

Manufacturing by Versa
Book design by Hana Anouk Nakamura
Production manager: Delaney Adams

ISBN 978-1-324-08394-8

Cataloging-in-Publication data is available from the Library of Congress.

W. W. Norton & Company, Inc., 500 Fifth Avenue, New York, NY 10110
www.wwnorton.com

W. W. Norton & Company Ltd., 15 Carlisle Street, London W1D 3BS

Authorized EU representative: EAS, Mustamäe tee 50, 10621 Tallinn, Estonia

1 2 3 4 5 6 7 8 9 0

REBELLIOUS
THE STORY OF
KEITH HARING
IN 12 PICTURES

Michael G. Long

NORTON YOUNG READERS
An Imprint of W. W. Norton & Company
Independent Publishers Since 1923

Author's Note

Keith Haring rarely titled his works. The chapter titles include either the given title or a short description of the chapter's lead picture. The second part of chapter titles refers to chapter content.

PROLOGUE

ILLEGAL

KEITH HOPPED OFF THE SUBWAY CAR, SCANNED THE AREA FOR cops, and made a beeline for his target—a sheet of black paper, about two feet by four feet, hanging between two advertisement posters.

He pulled a piece of chalk from his back pocket, crouched down, and began to draw two panels, or boxes, one on top of the other. His lines were smooth and bold, easy to see from a distance.

In the bottom panel, he drew a faceless human figure wielding a stick and chasing another human. The top panel depicted a human breaking the stick, as well as a heart enclosed in a circle.

It took only a minute or two to finish the whole thing.

What did it mean?

Keith didn't stick around to explain. Somewhere, at this subway stop or the next one, another empty black sheet beckoned him to keep drawing.

●   ●   ●

Then it happened.

A transit officer caught him red-handed, or better stated, white-fingered.

"You're under arrest for graffiti in the subway," the cop said, cuffing Keith's hands behind his back.

Keith didn't resist.

He had faced off with the police before, and he would do it again.

Rebellion was his thing.

Keith under arrest for criminal mischief, New York City subway, 1982.

1 RADIANT BABY

UNTITLED, 1990.

A CRAWLING, "RADIANT" BABY BECAME ONE OF KEITH'S BEST-KNOWN IMAGES, AND HE MADE IT HIS LOGO, OR SIGNATURE. AS A CHILD, KEITH LOVED DRAWING CARTOONS AND DREAMED OF BECOMING A CARTOONIST FOR THE WALT DISNEY COMPANY.

CHILDHOOD

IT STARTED BEFORE HE COULD WALK.

Allen Haring balanced his infant son on his lap and gave him a crayon. Less than a year old, Keith grabbed it with his tiny hand and started to scribble.

By the age of four, the little boy was filling his days with drawing.

"I could never get enough pencils and paper," his mother, Joan, said. "He'd go through tablets—and he'd draw on everything—everything, except the walls."

One day, he drew on the walls, too.

The kid had a rebellious streak.

If Keith wasn't drawing, he was watching TV at his grandmother's house.

The Harings lived in Kutztown, a small, quiet town in rural Pennsylvania, and Joan had no qualms about letting Keith walk alone to her mother's home, just a few blocks away.

The preschooler was all too happy to leave because he could ditch his mother's otherwise strict rules—like *No eating in front of the TV!* At Grandma's house, he could also watch all the TV he wanted.

Keith at seven months old, 1958.

One of his favorite shows was *Mister Ed*, starring a deep-voiced horse that cracked dry jokes, but the cartoons—*Looney Tunes, The Bugs Bunny Show, The Flintstones, The Jetsons*—captured his attention like nothing else.

Back home, Keith learned how to draw the cartoons he loved so much. Although his dad worked in electrical engineering, Allen was also an amateur artist who specialized in drawing funny creatures. He would draw a line on an empty piece of paper and invite Keith to do the same. Allen would then put down another line, and Keith would, too. After the back-and-forth continued for a bit, Allen would transform the lines into cartoon characters.

Keith was hooked by the madcap creatures—and by his dad's technique of using simple lines to make cartoons. Following Allen's example, Keith would make simple line drawings throughout his youth; he would become world famous for his "line" in his adult years.

Allen shared other important lessons, too. "Instead of teaching me to copy other cartoon characters or comics, he wanted me to invent my own characters," Keith recalled.

The young boy clearly took his dad's advice, and in the years ahead, he would famously invent crawling babies with no ears, barking dogs with no paws, and happy faces with three eyes.

For now, though, young Keith drew artistic inspiration from other innovative artists—like the wildly inventive Dr. Seuss.

Joan had her hands full with Keith's younger siblings, toddler Kay and baby Karen, as well as all the work required of a homemaker, but when she could steal away from the busyness, she and Keith would sit on the couch and read the tantalizing rhymes of Dr. Seuss.

By 1962, when Keith was four, Theodor Seuss Geisel had already penned some of his most popular titles, such as *The Cat in the Hat*, *How the Grinch Stole Christmas*, *Green Eggs and Ham*, and *The Sneeches and Other Stories*.

Allen also read to his young son.

"My father loved Dr. Seuss, and he'd read me those stories, and the way he read them to me was totally animated, which made me like them even more," Keith said. "So I was really into this array of Dr. Seuss characters, with their weirdness and absurdity."

"Perhaps in our drawing we were both influenced by the crazy drawings of Dr. Seuss," Allen said. "You could make cartoon characters go wild with the hair, hats, and noses."

Keith's picture of a clown on a horse, 1964.

There were other points of inspiration in young Keith's life—for example, a how-to-draw manual from the Walt Disney Company and Charles Schulz's drawings of Snoopy—but Allen was always the most significant influence, perhaps because he made drawing so much fun.

Sometimes, he and Keith would sit at the table, close their eyes, and begin drawing a figure they'd agreed on. They would have a vague sense of where their pens were moving on the page, but the lines would go this way and that, some connecting where they should and others branching into the oddest of places.

Then they would open their eyes and laugh out loud. The results were hilarious—and instructive. The game was "good practice for getting the rhythm of your hand and knowing where your hand is and what it's doing without watching, without seeing it," Allen said.

With guidance from his dad, Keith's youthful line was gradually becoming less herky-jerky and more fluid, all the better for drawing outlandish cartoons.

Kutztown Elementary was just down the street from the Haring home. All Keith had to do was walk out the back door and head straight.

Although he now had other subjects to study, Keith continued to obsess on drawing. "He was always drawing, drawing in school when he wasn't supposed to be," Allen said.

Keith did look up from his drawings long enough to notice the extraordinariness of his art teacher, Mrs. Blefgan. She had an artistic flair, a colorful way of being that was not typical in conservative, earth-toned Kutztown. She also hung groovy beads in her doorway and burned scented candles in her room.

"Her whole idea of being more extravagant or dressing differently gave me a first look at not being ordinary," Keith said.

But Keith wasn't exactly part of the pack, either.

"I had glasses from the time I was in second grade, so I was already sort of a little, you know, nerd."

He did not like sports. "He wasn't the type of kid who would grab a basketball and start shooting before gym class started," recalls classmate Bruce Koller. "He'd just stand there, waiting for the teacher."

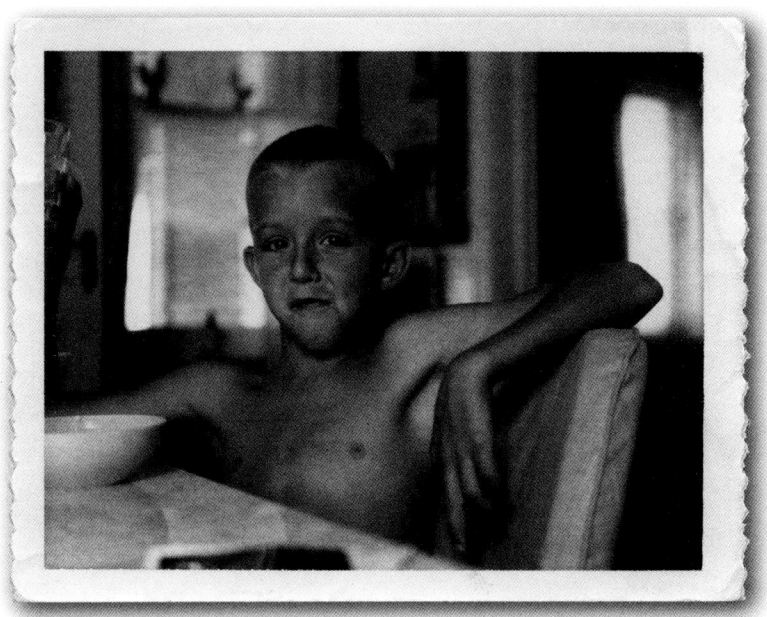

Keith's disinterest showed up in his skill level, which meant that he was often the last to be chosen for pickup teams. Although that made him feel "insecure," as he put it, he never tried to become an accomplished athlete.

Nor did he stay the course with the Kutztown boy scouts who learned to pitch tents, build campfires, and roast hot dogs, and he certainly didn't join the boys who shot squirrels to add to their family's dinner menu.

Allen (left), Keith, Kay, Joan, and Karen, Kutztown, 1964.

Some of those athletes, scouts, and hunters called Keith a "sissy." Not Bruce Koller, though. In later years, Keith said that Bruce was the only one who didn't make fun of him.

● ● ●

Art was Keith's first and only love, and in a fourth-grade essay, he shared just how much it meant to him.

"When I grow up I would like to be an artist in France," he wrote. "The reason is because I like to draw. I would get my money from the pictures I would sell. I hope I will be one."

But as he grew a bit older, Keith ditched France and dreamed instead of becoming a cartoonist for the Walt Disney Company. "I was really obsessed with Walt Disney a lot," he confessed. "I loved Walt Disney."

Kay (left), Keith, Karen, and their dog Mumbo, in their backyard, 1969.

Keith and Kutztown Elementary student Kermit Oswald had a lot in common and became best friends.

The two first met in a Sunday school class that Allen taught at St. John's United Church of Christ. During worship services, the friends would doodle on church bulletins and pass them back and forth, the sermon a distant echo.

Around sixth grade, the boys struck gold—they were given permission to set up their own art studio in a garage owned by Kermit's uncle and aunt. "It had a great upstairs, maple floors," Kermit says. "It was a pretty big room, like four hundred square feet, so we could go there and draw."

Although the two boys worked in the same space, in the garage and at school, they had dramatically different styles. Kermit drew realistic figures, while Keith stuck with imaginative cartoons.

In junior high school, Keith's favorite tool for drawing was the Rapidograph, a technical pen with a consistent ink flow. Lucy DeMatteo, his junior high school art teacher, said that Keith was stubborn when she asked him to try different tools and art forms.

I'd say, "Keith, why not try this or that," and he'd say, "I don't want to." Finally, I'd say, "OK, OK, do what you want."

But I wanted him to try different things. I wanted him to do an oil painting. I said, "Try it, Keith. It's another medium." Well, he tried it, but he never finished it. The point is, Keith only did what he wanted to do.

What he wanted to do was to draw cartoons, and now that he was out of elementary school, he also wanted to start inventing characters and scenes that went beyond the child-friendliness of Dr. Seuss and Walt Disney. An upcoming art show, organized by DeMatteo, gave him the opportunity.

Keith's contribution to the show was a fifteen-foot-long cartoon strip that showed hippies squaring off against the police and protesting for civil rights and women's rights. The general scene of people holding "Black Power" and "Women's Lib" protest signs was provocative enough in conservative Kutztown, but Keith had also drawn a female hippie baring her breasts.

DeMatteo was not amused. "[She] didn't make me take it out," Keith said. "But she was mad, and it was a scandal."

More scandals were on the way, and all of them stemmed from Keith's developing distaste for the conventional beliefs that filled his home and hometown.

KEITH'S LINE

An artist's line is the mark that joins together different parts, or points, in their drawings. One art teacher says that "a simple way of thinking of a line is to imagine a point that moves."

Lines can be thick or thin, short or long, and straight or circular. Artists often use them to outline their subject, detail the subject's features, and add texture and shade.

Sometimes an artist has a markedly distinct, or unique, line. If you look at Keith's outline of the cartoonish images he drew in his twenties, you can see that it's usually thick and bold.

According to art curator and dealer Jeffrey Deitch, "Keith Haring's line has a strength and confidence that is immediately recognizable. His line is like a signature—you can see only a section of his drawing and know that it is Keith's hand. The line of a great artist is like the tone of a great violinist—unique and instantly recognizable. Keith's line also had a rhythm, like the movement of a dancer—always exact and perfectly placed."

Painter and writer Brion Gysin said that Keith's line "is a carved line like the one man made . . . in the back of the cave."

Keith drawing his distinctive line in the New York City subway, 1983.

2 ROCK BANDS

UNTITLED, NO DATE [1974—1975].

Abstract shapes, bright psychedelic color, and the names of rock bands: As a teen, Keith adopted attitudes and actions that ran contrary to his hometown's conservative values.

TEENS

JOAN HARING THOUGHT THE UNITED STATES WOULD HAVE BEEN better off had the Beatles never landed there. "I distinctly remember hearing my mother say that the boat that brought over the Beatles should have sunk," Keith said.

So Joan probably sniffed at the band manufactured in their image—the Monkees.

In 1966, *The Monkees* premiered as a television sitcom featuring the zany adventures of a British boy band. But the Monkees were a successful band in real life, too, even outselling the Beatles, with three No. 1 hit songs in 1966 and 1967.

Guess who loved them?

Keith adored the Monkees. As a fourth grader, he was so enamored that he commandeered a wig and hosted a pretend Monkees gig in his backyard.

Joan must have rolled her eyes.

Conservative citizens across the country looked askance at the Monkees, partly because they did not fit into traditional gender roles. Unlike most Kutztown boys, with their close-cropped hair and straight jeans, the Monkees grew their hair long and wore bell-bottoms, beaded necklaces, and silk shirts and scarves. The band members were also downright silly and loud—not exactly the kind of boys who made stealthy squirrel hunters.

Keith couldn't run fast enough to buy *16* and *Tiger Beat*, the teen magazines that splashed the Monkees on their covers. It was unusual for a Kutztown boy to purchase these. Their pulsating headlines promised secret pictures, including a "Kolossal Kolor Pin-Up," and Keith found them irresistible.

He didn't just swoon over the photos—he also used them to create art. "I would cut out the pictures of the Monkees, especially Davy Jones, who was the cute, young one. I'd cut these pictures out and make collages and books."

Keith's obsession with the Monkees marked one of the first times he truly worried his parents, particularly his father. But this wasn't the only gender-related issue to raise his parents' eyebrows.

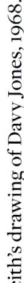
Keith's drawing of Davy Jones, 1968.

In 1967, boys in Kutztown played with G.I. Joe dolls and carried metal lunchboxes that showed the pretend soldier wielding a knife and a machine gun. He was on the hunt, and not for animals.

Although Keith enjoyed his G.I. Joe, he was much more captivated by Ken, Barbie's slim, blue-eyed, blond boyfriend, and by the couple's glamorous life. Rather than crawling through jungles and killing people, Ken and Barbie drove a convertible and listened to groovy music at the beach.

Keith asked his mother for a Ken doll, but she flat out refused. So Keith turned to his indulgent grandmother, and she agreed. Of course her grandson could play with a doll made for girls.

Like the Monkees, the Ken doll of the 1960s wore fashionable bell-bottoms, and Keith craved a pair for himself.

But Joan was having none of that, either. Keith grew even more peeved when his mother dragged him to a store where the bargain-basement clothes were nothing like Ken's.

Ever stubborn and rebellious, Keith assumed control of his clothes whenever and wherever possible. While attending a church camp far from Joan's watchful eyes, he even ditched them.

"I must have been eleven or twelve, and for the talent show, I decided I'd do a striptease number as a woman," he recalled. "I remember we built a fake cake out of cardboard, and I came out of the cake. Some girls helped me with the makeup—and we had striptease music. So I did this striptease, but I didn't take off *all* of my clothes because this was a church camp."

• • •

While Keith was dabbling in gender-bending, Joan and Allen attempted to shield him from other attitudes and actions that ran counter to Kutztown's conventional life. When the TV news reported on controversial issues, for instance, they sent him out of the living room.

Keith in his hippie stage, 1976.

Annoyed, Keith went to his grandmother's house and watched TV freely, without censorship, and read her glossy magazines, *Life* and *Look*, where he encountered the civil rights movement, the Vietnam War, and an uprising of young people, including hippies, who criticized racism and authoritarianism, militarism and materialism, and conventionality in fashion, sex, and religion.

It didn't take long for Keith to realize that his parents were far removed from this countercultural America. Middle class and conservative, Joan and Allen were part of conventional America—and enthusiastic supporters of President Richard Nixon. They backed the Vietnam War, a law-and-order response to social unrest, traditional fashion, heterosexuality over homosexuality, and weekly church attendance.

"I never really felt a part of that," Keith said.

Keith expressed his dissent from conventionality in that scandalous cartoon strip he drew for the junior high school arts show—the one with bare breasts.

At the age of fifteen, he took another step away from mainstream Kutztown—he transformed himself from a nerd into something like a hippie. He grew his hair long and began wearing ripped jeans and T-shirts.

At a Halloween party in 1973, he tried drugs for the first time, a marijuana cigarette that left him feeling disoriented and yet also craving more. He soon turned to whatever else he could get his hands on—speed, quaaludes, and angel dust (PCP).

Leaving behind his best friend Kermit, Keith started hanging out with other druggies and hippie-wannabees. They huddled in his bedroom, got high, and blasted rock music by Led Zeppelin, Lynyrd Skynyrd, and Black Sabbath.

"Turn that racket down!" Joan often yelled. According to daughter Karen, Joan and Allen preferred the military marching songs composed by John Philip Sousa.

Keith usually drew during these bedroom get-togethers, and his new playlist served as source material. Using colored felt-tip pens, he made posters filled with stylized names of the rock groups, as well as cool hippie iconography, like rainbows and flowers.

He and his friends also went to Grateful Dead concerts. Venerated by hippies across the country, the Dead were notorious for their use of hallucinogenic drugs such as LSD, and for psychedelic songs that combined elements of jazz, folk, and rock.

Keith first took LSD, also known as acid, in the relative safety of his bedroom. During that first psychedelic trip, he sat at the drawing table that his father had made for him.

"I started doing abstract shapes," he explained. "I started doing stream-of-consciousness drawing and shapes melting one into another. And then really figuring out the way the shapes fit together and building this structure of complex drawings, where one thing leads to another."

Entranced by this new abstract style, Keith developed it further in his high school art class, in a corner where he worked alone. His art teacher, Nita Dietrich, was all-around impressed.

"I was really fascinated by him," she said. "He loved pen and ink, and he worked so intricately! His sense of proportion and his patterns just intrigued me! The way the patterns would carry you through and around and in and out. He had such imagination."

Abstract shapes in a puzzle that Keith made for his sister, Karen, in his teens, 1974–1976.

Keith's move into abstraction meant leaving behind at least some of his representational art—his drawings of recognizable figures. It also led to a major shift in the way he thought of himself and his art.

Dispensing with his childhood dream of becoming a cartoonist with the Walt Disney Company, he now wanted to become a *fine artist*—someone whose art would be creative and intellectual, serious and meaningful, and appreciated by art critics.

Although Keith excelled in art class, his life was otherwise a mess.

"I was a terror when I was a teenager," he recalled.

He stole alcohol from the local fire company, shoplifted at local businesses, and skipped school. His grades tanked because he was drinking alcohol and smoking pot before the classes he did attend. Under the influence, he once told the principal that he was late because "terrorist rabbits" had taken him prisoner.

After school and on weekends, his friend Penny Wagner would pick him up in her Volkswagen Bug, and they would drive through the countryside, smoking pot with the windows up, no matter how hot it was, to enhance the drug's effects. Penny found Keith "very sweet, very kind, sarcastically funny—and kind of lost."

Joan and Allen were distraught. They set new rules and boundaries for their son, even denying him permission to get his driver's license.

But nothing worked.

Then, in the summer before his senior year, Keith ran away. Hitching a ride with some friends, he headed to Long Beach Island, New Jersey, with no plan other than to get the hell out of Kutztown.

At the beach, Keith was confronted with a new reality—he had to take care of himself. By his own account, he flourished, finding a job as a dishwasher, meeting lots of new people, and refining his abstract art. He also became more selective in his use of illegal drugs, dropping those that scared him to death, like angel dust, and using only those that he considered less dangerous, like pot.

As summer vacation ended, Keith packed his bags and returned to Kutztown for his senior year.

Joan and Allen were relieved when their son walked through the front door—and when they sensed he had matured during his time away. Keith was happy, too, and he even shed a few tears.

Settling back into home life, he got his driver's license and committed himself to earning the grades required for high school graduation. He and

Kermit reconnected. The two best friends returned to hanging out, making art, and discussing their favorite artists.

Although Keith got his "shit together," as he put it, he did not change his attitude toward the traditional beliefs and practices espoused by his parents and his hometown.

Keith drew abstract squiggles in this picture of a pothead, 1975.

He still smoked pot and dropped acid, he still dressed like a hippie, and he still skipped school.

He skipped gym class so much that he was in danger of not graduating, so when the high school office called Joan one day to inform her that Keith was absent, she gathered up Kristen, Keith's youngest sister, jumped in the car, and sped toward the woods, up by the reservoir, where Keith and his fellow truants usually hung out.

"I don't know how she knew where to go, but Keith got *delivered* to school," Kristen remembers.

Back on the road to graduation, Keith began to plan for life after high school.

While he longed to become a fine artist, he followed a conventional recommendation made by the cautious adults in his life.

"Being under the influence of parents and guidance counselors, I was convinced that if I was going to make a living as [a fine] artist, I had to do commercial art"— the type of art that companies used to promote themselves and their products.

Keith wasn't too hip to the idea, but in the late spring of his senior year, he decided to visit the Ivy School of Professional Art in Pittsburgh.

The trip would be revelatory.

MORE Than a TERROR

Karen DeLong, Keith's middle sister, remembers that her brother wasn't just a terror in his teen years—he was also sweet and thoughtful.

It was my eleventh or twelfth birthday.

The day was rainy and warm, and Keith was wearing the yellow rain slicker that he wore when he had to deliver the newspaper in the rain.

He was on his bicycle, and he came up [to the house] and said, "I have a present for you!"

I was like, "Ohhhh! What is it?"

He reached into his pocket and pulled out this tiny little kitten.

"Happy birthday!"

He knew I loved animals, and I said, "This is the best birthday present ever!" But Mom was allergic to cats, and she said, "Nope—the cat's not staying."

So I played with it for a few hours, and then Keith took it back to the owner. Even though I had it for just a short time, it was the best gift ever.

3 EMBRACING COUPLE

UNTITLED, 1987.

ENERGY AND LOVE RADIATING FROM HUMAN FIGURES IN AN EMBRACE. AFTER HE CAME OUT AS A GAY MAN, KEITH OFTEN DREW AND PAINTED IMAGES THAT CELEBRATED LOVE, PHYSICAL AFFECTION, AND SEX.

COMING OUT

KEITH LIKED GIRLS.

During his summer getaway to Long Beach Island, he and his friends frequented the local shopping mall in search of girls they might hook up with. While his friends succeeded, Keith failed.

The mounting rejections stung, not just because they added to his insecure feelings about his looks, but also because he desperately wanted to lose his virginity.

Throughout high school, Keith satisfied himself with assistance from magazines like *Penthouse* and *Playboy*.

Penthouse included pictures of men having sex with women, and Keith paid attention to the male bodies just as much as he did to the female ones. "But I always knew I was *supposed* to be with a girl," he said.

Traditional morality, in Kutztown and across the country, reserved its blessing for heterosexual sex within marriage. Although Keith had no desire to abide by the marriage requirement, he was *not* planning to buck conventional beliefs about heterosexuality.

But, alas, no young women showed interest in him—until a fateful trip to Pittsburgh.

In the spring of his senior year, Keith and a friend hitchhiked to Pittsburgh to check out the Ivy School of Professional Art. They arranged to stay at another friend's rambling farm outside the city. The comfortable lodgings included a heated pool, but for Keith, the best part of the visit, hands down, was meeting Susan Kriske.

Susan was Keith's age, she was fun-loving, and she had a hippie sensibility. She also found Keith cute. The attraction was mutual, and by the end of the first night, Keith and Susan were swimming in the pool.

And then it happened—Keith was no longer a virgin.

After visiting Ivy, Keith returned home and finalized his plans to attend Ivy in the fall.

He stayed in close touch with Susan, too. The two teens became a couple, visited each other during the summer months, and fell in love. "I always knew that I could make someone fall in love with me if they saw some other side of me," Keith said.

At the end of the summer, Keith was raring to leave Kutztown. "The first thing I wanted to do was to get out of that little town."

With a few bags in tow, he dashed off for Pittsburgh.

Susan and Keith about to hitchhike to Pittsburgh, 1978.

Keith did *not* fall in love with Ivy, to say the least. His abstract style was a poor fit for the school's practical focus on graphic design, advertising, and illustration. Keith's ongoing dream was to become a *fine artist,* not someone who worked in commercial art during the day and then did his own art whenever he could squeeze it in. Rather than making the best of Ivy, Keith quickly identified it as an obstruction to his dream.

During Christmas break, he read a book that gave him more fodder for rejecting commercial art—*The Art Spirit.* Author Robert Henri had a high-minded view of art in general and drawing in particular. "Your drawing should be an expression of your spiritual sight," he wrote. "You should not draw a line, but an inspired line." For Henri, art wasn't a commercial job—it was a spiritual practice.

After just six months of studies, Keith ditched Ivy. "I would not prostitute [my] talents by doing commercial art," he later explained.

Tapping into their hippie spirit, Keith and Susan decided to hitchhike to California, with a plan to check out art schools for Keith and attend Grateful Dead concerts.

A page from Keith's journal of his trip to California, May 1977.

Keith was still a Deadhead, and his backpack displayed the group's striking logo, a skull with a lightning bolt through it, but adorned with Keith's tiny, intricate, abstract shapes. He also stuffed his pack with silk-screened T-shirts that he and Susan hoped to sell to concertgoers.

The trip was great fun, and in May 1977, the couple arrived in San Francisco and found a place where they could sleep and eat for free.

"The guy who ran it was gay, I think," Keith wrote in his journal, referring to the minister who directed the shelter.

After dinner, the director's male assistant took the visiting couple on a walk through the Castro, a neighborhood humming with gay men. Using a slur for gay men that was commonplace at the time, Keith noted that he "saw more faggots than I saw in my entire life."

One of those gay men was right next to him, and when he finally figured out the assistant was hitting on him, he drew closer to Susan's side. Still, something vaguely familiar was stirring within him, and he was finally beginning to pay it serious attention.

"Little by little it became obvious to me that while I was still sleeping with Suzy, I'd been fantasizing more about men."

Keith and Susan completed their exploration of art schools, and since they were running out of money and had no other plans, they headed back to Pittsburgh. Susan took a job making health-food sandwiches, and after a period of being on welfare, Keith landed work as an assistant cook, then as a custodian at the Pittsburgh Arts and Crafts Center.

The couple soon began to drift apart. Susan started to see someone else, and Keith found himself longing to act on his gay fantasies. At first, he just poked around Pittsburgh's gay life, but one evening, feeling rather desperate, he walked into a gay bar with the sole purpose of having sex with a man—any man—before the night was over.

And that's what he did.

Keith's first experience did not leave him feeling warm and fuzzy, or even fully satisfied. "I didn't even really like it," he recalled.

But his experiences improved as he dove into other gay bars, including a Brown and Black nightclub called the Temper Trap. Keith's growing encounters confirmed his sense that he was a gay man and that gay sex was for him.

"I knew *that* was what I was supposed to be doing in the first place," he said.

Did Keith's growing recognition of his gay sexuality affect his life as an artist?

He did not substantially change his style at this point. He continued to make "pseudo-Abstract Expressionist" (his words) works inspired by Jackson Pollock and other abstract artists.

But the period of coming out in Pittsburgh did coincide with a dramatic increase in the size of Keith's abstract art and a broadening of his artistic vision. Influenced by an artist named Pierre Alechinsky, Keith now used big brushes to apply acrylics to large sheets of paper.

Keith in front of his abstract painting, Pittsburgh, 1978.

He was also influenced by an artist named Christo, who was famous for creating *Running Fence*, a nylon curtain that spanned almost twenty-five miles in northern California. Impressed with the way Christo's art attracted everyday people, Keith started to think about making art for people who typically did not visit museums and galleries.

On June 30, 1978, Keith opened a one-man show at the Pittsburgh Arts and Crafts Center, where he had earlier finagled a basement studio and captured the attention of the center's director.

With his broadened artistic vision, Keith made sure the invitation list included not only Pittsburgh's high-art class, but also his new friends, including lots of LGBTQ and Black and Brown folks he had met in bars and clubs.

Keith was thrilled to see such a diverse crowd on opening night.

Keith's coming out hastened the end of his two-year relationship with Susan. The split did not prove easy. Keith later depicted it as horrible, with loud fighting in the streets. He also claimed that Susan was pregnant at the time and that he faced a choice of splitting up and leaving town or marrying her and becoming a father.

In her own memories of the breakup, Susan makes it sound much less dramatic. "It was sad for both of us," she says. "But it was fine. It just happened. It was what it was." And no, she adds, she was *not* pregnant, and she did *not* tell Keith that she was pregnant.

In August 1978, Keith bolted for New York City, claiming that he had gotten all he could out of Pittsburgh and that the city's art crowd wasn't quite up to his standards.

"I wasn't finding any other people my age or close to my age that were totally committed to being an artist or were making anything new and committed to it."

Plus, he had applied and been accepted to the School of Visual Arts on Manhattan's East Twenty-Third Street, a place where he could develop his skills as a fine artist.

"I wanted intensity for my art, and I wanted intensity for my life," he said.

Manhattan would not disappoint.

4. CLONES GO HOME

CLONES GO HOME, 1980.

ONE OF KEITH'S FIRST PIECES OF STREET ART, STENCILED AT AN INTERSECTION ON THE DIVIDING LINE BETWEEN NEW YORK'S EAST AND WEST VILLAGE NEIGHBORHOODS. IN THE EAST VILLAGE, KEITH FOUND GAY MEN WHO WEREN'T LIKE THE PREPPIE "GAY CLONES" OF THE WEST VILLAGE. KEITH'S ART BECAME LESS ABSTRACT AND MORE REALISTIC WHEN HE STARTED TO USE HIS SEXUALITY AS SUBJECT MATERIAL.

NEW YORK CITY

ON HIS FIRST DAY IN MANHATTAN, KEITH STROLLED DOWN
Christopher Street in Greenwich Village, where gay men were here, there, and everywhere.

"It was like landing in a candy store or, better, a gay Disneyland!" he said.

Tasting with his eyes, Keith walked on until he arrived at the Christopher Street Pier overlooking the Hudson River. The dilapidated pier was full of scantily clad gay men basking in the sun or even making out.

Keith was gobsmacked. He met another gay man and went back to his apartment. The two got along so well that within forty-eight hours, Keith became the man's roommate, though as a friend rather than a partner.

Their small apartment was smack dab in the heart of the West Village—the city's epicenter for gay life—and light-years from Pittsburgh.

Although Keith was excited about the School of Visual Arts (SVA) and its focus on the fine arts, the fit was far from perfect. In a class on painting and color, he

Keith painting an abstract work at the School of Visual Arts, 1978.

resisted using oils and canvases, the traditional tools of "serious" painters.

He also rebelled in a class taught by Barbara Schwartz. When she instructed her students to draw a realistic representation of a human model, Keith refused, choosing instead to draw an abstract interpretation.

Barbara Schwartz, left, and Keith, center, at the School of Visual Arts, 1978.

"Keith was having none of it," recalls classmate John Imbro. "He told me in one conversation that he *couldn't* draw like that and he had no desire to learn."

● ● ●

But Schwartz and Keith took a liking to each other, and Keith used her assignments as occasions for coming out in his art—for depicting his sexual life in his drawings.

And what a life it was. Most nights, he took advantage of gay bars like Ninth Circle, International Stud, and Anvil, where encounters in backrooms and bathrooms were readily available.

For Schwartz's class, Keith filled a notebook with sketches of seventy penises, including his own. The drawings marked a notable shift from his earlier focus on abstract designs. "All those little abstract shapes I was doing became completely phallic," he explained.

The drawings also embodied a new approach to coming out. No longer content to be quiet, Keith was now direct, in your face, confrontational. Sharing his phallic drawings at SVA became "a way to assert my sexuality, and to force people to deal with it," he said.

Keith presented his erotically charged art in other classes, too. In Keith Sonnier's class on art, performance, and media, he created uncensored videos of his own naked body. Sonnier was delighted with the work, but its graphic content scandalized some of the students.

Keith didn't care.

He was out—*deal with it*.

SVA student Kenny Scharf received a sheet of graph paper with half of it, the right side, filled with hundreds of tiny penises.

Although most were instantly recognizable, they were also a tiny bit abstract. Some looked like birds or airplanes, some phalluses had five testicles, and some testicles looked like hearts.

Kenny—who loved Keith's fun personality and his fierce resolve to do whatever he wanted—kept the drawing for decades.

Near the end of 1978, Keith and Drew Staub, a friend from Kutztown, moved into an apartment in the East Village.

Unlike the West Village, the East Village did not have a refined feel. Landlords had allowed their buildings to crumble, and entire blocks looked as if they had been bombed. Drugs were plentiful, and crime was common, night and day.

But rents were low.

Because the down-and-dirty neighborhood was so affordable, it attracted artists, writers, and musicians, and became fertile ground for a creative revolution in the 1970s and 1980s.

With little money in their pockets, Keith and Drew fit right in.

Just across the street from Drew and Keith's new apartment was Club Baths, a gay bathhouse that catered to men seeking pleasure. For five dollars, customers would receive a towel and a locker. After disrobing, they would wrap the towel around their waist and cruise hallways and rooms in search of a partner.

Keith dove headfirst into the club, especially on Monday and Friday nights, when two customers, if they presented themselves as buddies, could gain admission for the price of one. Keith discovered that he far preferred gay bathhouses over gay bars.

"First of all, everyone at the baths was sort of on an equal level," he explained. "I mean, everyone was just wearing a towel, so you were not judged by what you were wearing, and there would not be the same attitude you encountered at the bars."

Keith and Drew had not talked openly about their sexuality before moving in together, but one night, the roommates ran into each other at Club Baths.

Surprise!

"We were like, 'Oh, hi!'" Drew recalls.

The two continued to bump into each other at the club, but they chose to stay just friends and not become involved. But now that their secret was out in the open, Keith felt free to decorate their kitchen wall with phallic drawings galore.

In June 1980, Keith took part in *The Times Square Show*, an exhibit organized by a cooperative of up-and-coming artists, many from the East Village. The show was held in an abandoned massage parlor and featured the works of about one hundred artists.

In his assigned space, Keith exhibited *Art Sin Boy*—sheets of copy paper with thirteen typed letters in numerous combinations ("sin as if," "if boy sin," and "fat art is," for example). The complicated wordplay was the result of inspiration he had drawn from Brion Gysin and William S. Burroughs, innovative writers known for cutting up texts and then rearranging the words to make a new, and sometimes unintelligible, text.

Visitors would not have to look too closely to see that some of Keith's phrases sounded gay themes, but to make the connection to gayness even stronger, he drew phalluses all over the surrounding wall space.

Penises were appearing everywhere in Keith's art, including in works he displayed at an eccentric nightclub in the basement of a Polish church in the East Village.

Managed by the artist Ann Magnuson, Club 57 featured monster movies and art films, poetry readings and plays, and art shows and theme nights, like Putt-Putt Reggae Night, when customers could play miniature golf to reggae music. Beer and psychedelic drugs and go-go dancing were also part of the scene.

Early on, Keith did poetry readings at the club, but after numerous appearances on stage, he came to realize that poetry, despite his prodigious output and professed love, wasn't his specialty. A cascade of booing from veteran poets probably helped expedite his exit.

Keith turned his attention to organizing art shows at the club. With Magnuson's support, he curated a one-night show that displayed a wide variety of works from sixty different artists. Other shows followed, the most popular in February 1981—the *Club 57 First Annual Group Erotic and Pornographic Art Exhibition*.

The advertising poster for the event was designed by Keith's good friend, John McLaughlin, also known as John Sex, a gay, fun-loving, and super-talented SVA student. John's suggestive work showed a naked man standing with a model airplane between his legs.

Inside the exhibit, guests were treated to works with equally fantastical and gay themes. A giant silver phallus hung from the ceiling, for example, and a drawing by local artist David Wojnarowicz depicted a naked man with a dog's head.

The provocative show attracted the attention of established art collectors and received a positive review from the *SoHo Weekly News*. The writer also described Keith as "a cutie" with "a great underplayed look."

Keith and his friend, photographer Tseng Kwong Chi, reading poetry at Club 57, 1980.

● ● ●

An underplayed look? What did *that* mean?

Perhaps it meant that Keith wasn't like the West Village "clones," as they were derisively called, who cloaked themselves in Lacoste shirts and sweaters, colorful chinos, and boat shoes or loafers. Rebelling against the preppy look, Keith stuck to straight-cut jeans, T-shirts, and sneakers.

Or perhaps it meant that he did not visit the same expensive hair stylists used by the West Villagers. His hair was now short and a bit ratty.

Whatever it meant, the compliment no doubt sat well with Keith, who never saw himself as fetching and was often frustrated over his failure to attract beautiful young men.

Gay art would remain Keith's stock-in-trade for years to come.

So in 1988, organizers of the first National Coming Out Day knew exactly where to turn for help in spreading word about the inaugural event. Keith accepted their invitation, and his colorful poster showed a human figure bursting out of a closet and dancing joyfully—just as he did when first arriving in Greenwich Village.

Interestingly, by the time the poster appeared in public, Keith still had not fully come out to his parents, at least not in a way that said, "Mom and Dad, I'm gay."

NATIONAL COMING OUT DAY...

OCTOBER 11-1988 NATIONAL GAY RIGHTS ADVOCATES

Keith created the first poster for National Coming Out Day, 1988.

Keith explained the dynamic between him and his parents in the last year of his life. "My parents have been so amazing about the whole thing [his sexuality], but in their own way—knowing but not saying anything. I never tried to hide it from them, and they never asked me about it."

But that did not mean they were always comfortable with his sexuality—or with his gay-themed drawings.

In September 1987, Keith attended a festive and popular exhibit of his art back in Kutztown.

By this point, he had grown to appreciate his hometown, but he still couldn't help but sound a note of rebellion. So when a young man handed him a large inflatable Gumby to sign, Keith gave the cartoon character a significantly sized phallus.

Joan Haring caught her son in the act.

"*Keeeeith!*" she said. "This is *not* New York!"

Keith grinned—and kept on drawing.

But Keith usually made sure that his public art, or art that he made in public, was suitable for a wide audience.

His self-censorship had begun in earnest in 1980 when he grabbed a piece of chalk and drew on a black panel hanging on a subway wall. The G-rated drawing would be seen by thousands of everyday people, including children.

It would also change his life.

5 HUMAN ON DOLPHIN

UNTITLED, 1982.

Three of Keith's favorite images: a dolphin, a human in motion, and a glowing stick in a subway drawing at New York's 51st Street Station. Influenced by graffiti, Keith drew in the streets and subway, hoping to attract an audience largely ignored by the art world. Subway riders often stopped to ask him about the meaning of his drawings.

GRAFFITI

KEITH FOUND THE JOB DESCRIPTION TO BE "QUITE BIZARRE," AND perhaps for that very reason, he called the number listed in the "help wanted" section.

Before long, he was part of a crew cutting wildflowers along New Jersey's highways. The crew's boss would then sell the freely harvested flowers to florists and stores across Manhattan.

The job provided Keith with prolonged periods for contemplation. At breaktime, he would sit among the gorgeous flowers and think about his life as an artist.

In those quiet moments, two things became clear: He longed to devote more time to drawing and painting, and he wanted to adopt a style that would speak to everyday people.

"More than anything, I wanted to communicate!" he said.

Keith's desire to communicate with a wider public stemmed partly from his first year at the School of Visual Arts, when he worked in a studio that opened onto Twenty-Second Street.

"I was drawing on enormous rolls of photo backdrop paper that I'd spread out on the floor, and people walking by would come in to watch," he recalled. "Most of them weren't the type that go to art galleries, but a lot of their comments struck me as more perceptive than those of my teachers and fellow students."

The experience convinced him that the art world should stop naval-gazing and start paying attention to everyday people. As he put this in his journal,

The public has a right to art.

The public is being ignored by most contemporary artists.

The public needs art, and it is the responsibility of a "self-proclaimed artist" to realize the public needs art, and not to make bourgeois art for the few and ignore the masses.

Art is for everybody.

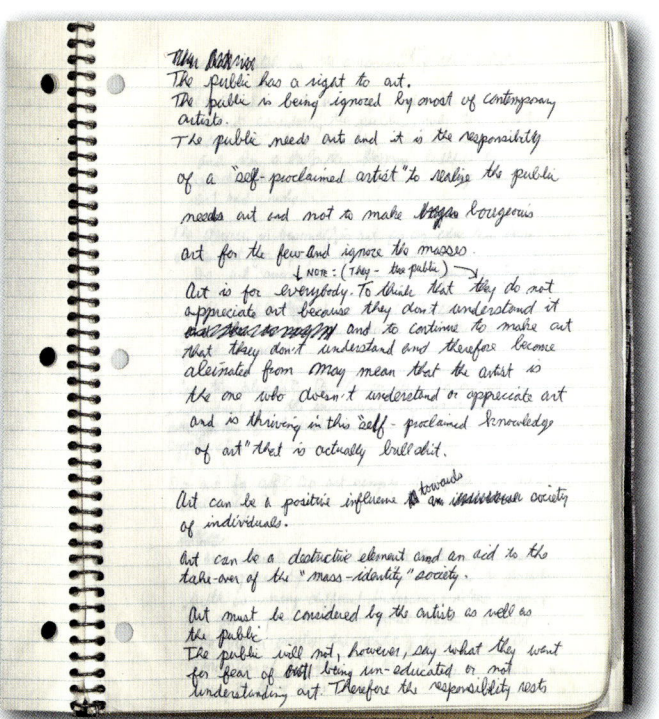

The public has a right to art.
The public is being ignored by most of contemporary artists.
The public needs art and it is the responsibility of a "self-proclaimed artist" to realize the public needs art and not to make ~~bogus~~ bourgeois art for the few and ignore the masses.
↳ NOTE : (they - the public)
Art is for everybody. To think that they do not appreciate art because they don't understand it ~~and they don't~~ and to continue to make art that they don't understand and therefore become alienated from may mean that the artist is the one who doesn't understand or appreciate art and is thriving in this "self-proclaimed knowledge of art" that is actually bullshit.

Art can be a positive influence ~~towards~~ an ~~~~ society of individuals.

Art can be a destructive element and an aid to the take-over of the "mass-identity" society.

Art must be considered by the artists as well as the public.
The public will not, however, say what they want for fear of ~~being~~ being un-educated or not understanding art. Therefore the responsibility rests

After his wildflower epiphany, Keith borrowed a friend's studio, and in a two-day frenzy, he drew and painted a series of new images—spaceships, four-legged animals, human figures, and dolphins.

The images looked cartoonish, and each seemed to represent, or stand for, something bigger than itself.

"I was thinking of these images as symbols, as a vocabulary of things," Keith said. The spaceships, for instance, hinted at powerful forces beyond human control.

When combined, the images also seemed to depict an event, tell a story, or share a message.

Keith was delighted with the results. Not only had he returned to his love of cartoons—he had also begun to create a visual language for communicating with the public. In fact, Keith believed that because the images embodied information, they themselves "demanded to be in public."

On July 21, 1980, Keith showed this new work at Club 57. While he was pleased with the positive feedback, he really wanted to take his images far beyond the small club.

But how to do that?

Traditional avenues for spreading art—galleries and museums—weren't viable options. Keith's work wasn't well-known, and dealers and curators weren't out looking for him.

So Keith turned to a group long ignored by the art world—the graffiti writers, or artists, who used the streets and subways as their canvas.

Following the example of graffiti writers, Keith made one of the most fateful decisions of his life—he grabbed a black marker and hit the streets.

Strolling through Lower Manhattan, he noticed that the four-sided base of a metal light pole was empty.

Keith in front of his new symbolic images, 1980.

Aha!

Keith crouched down and began drawing.

"The first image on the street was the crawling person," he said later. "At the time, I was thinking of it as a person crawling around on all fours."

He then moved on to other light poles and construction walls and kiosks, any surface that worked well for his marker and was not already taken by another writer.

The second image he drew was a four-legged animal. "In the beginning it looked like it could have been a cow or a sheep or a horse."

As he continued drawing in the days ahead, his images morphed. The animal began to look like a dog, and the crawling people began to have bigger heads and resemble babies. He also started drawing more babies than dogs, and in short order, the crawling baby became his street signature—his very own tag.

● ● ●

A crawling baby?

The unique tag generated a loud buzz among the city's graffiti writers, including Fred "Fab 5 Freddy" Brathwaite.

Keith's crawling baby tag, 1981.

Keith had first met Fab and another famous writer, Lee Quiñones, at *The Times Square Show*, in a room where the writers' paintings were on display. Without knowing who the two men were, Keith told them that the paintings were by Fab and Lee, important figures in the graffiti movement.

Amused, the graffiti duo looked at each other.

Then, a friend walked into the room and called them by name.

"Keith was mortified," Fab recalled.

But that uncomfortable, and comical, moment led to a lasting friendship between Fab and Keith, with the two bonding over their mutual love of graffiti, dance clubs, and the emerging hip-hop scene.

It was Fab more than anyone else who introduced Keith to the wider graffiti community and helped him earn the respect of the streets.

As the summer of 1980 ended, Keith met with Jean Siegel, the head of the fine arts department at the School of Visual Arts, to talk about the upcoming fall semester. Their conversation took an unexpected turn while Keith was relaying news about his recent work.

Keith and Fred "Fab 5 Freddy" Braithwaite outside Club 57, 1980.

"All of a sudden, it dawned on me! What am I doing going to school? I was totally hooked up in the underground art scene. . . . Furthermore, I was discovering my *own* work in a way that was just starting to totally explode."

Keith dropped out of SVA.

In late 1980, the art school dropout moved into a two-story loft on Fortieth Street, near Times Square, with his best friend and fellow artist, Kenny Scharf. To cover his living expenses, Keith took a job at the Mudd Club, a nightclub known for being cool in a black-clothes sort of way.

One day, while taking the subway to work, Keith noticed a Christmas advertisement for Johnnie Walker Red Label Scotch. Featured in various subway stations, the poster showed an old redbrick train station with a snowy landscape in the foreground.

Aha!

Keith pulled a black marker out of his pocket and drew a row of crawling babies in the snow and a spaceship zapping them from above. Surrounded by rays, the crawling babies were now radiant babies.

Keith on the street in New York, 1978–1979.

Keith was stoked. It was one thing to draw babies on the streets of Lower Manhattan, but it was quite another to draw them in a subway station used by millions of people from across the world.

What could be better than that?

Near the end of December 1980, Keith walked through his usual subway entrance and spotted something he hadn't noticed before—advertising panels without advertisements.

"The panels were covered with a soft matte black paper, which was *dying* to be drawn on," he recalled.

Rushing back up the subway steps, Keith hurried up the street, found a stationery store, bought a box of white chalk, dashed back to the empty panel, and drew on it.

"It felt incredible!"

Keith drawing in the New York City subway, 1983. *Art in Transit* would be the title of a 1984 book of his subway drawings.

For years, the panels with expired ads had been covered with black paper until the next ad appeared. They had escaped Keith's full attention, but now he started to see them everywhere.

At first, he drew only on his way to work, but the experience became so rewarding that he soon went to the subway with the sole purpose of drawing. Traveling from station to station, he found numerous panels just waiting for him to draw on them.

After a week or so, Keith mentioned the drawings to his close friend, photographer Tseng Kwong Chi, who immediately decided to take pictures of them. It proved to be exhausting work because Keith sometimes made thirty to forty drawings in a single day—a staggering output of creativity.

The subway experience fulfilled Keith's dream of taking his art to the masses.

Countless subway riders watched him draw, and some even stopped to ask him about a particular drawing.

"What does it mean?"

The question made sense because some of the drawings were cryptic. At one and the same time, they looked both realistic and abstract. There were mermaids with wings, dogs with massive jaws, box-shaped heads with three eyes, and human figures with TV heads.

Keith on the New York City subway, and one of his drawings on the wall, 1983.

Keith typically refused to answer questions about their meaning. "That's your part," he replied. "I only do the drawings."

And sure enough, some riders would share their views. "They'd go off and tell me stories and their interpretations, and it would be much better than what I could have told them anyway," Keith said.

But the more he drew in the subway, the more deliberate he became about guiding the public toward specific messages that he wanted them to grasp—for example, messages about peace and love.

On occasion, he broke his own rules and publicly shared the meaning of some of his images. The stick, he said, meant "domination, power, and aggression," and the "babies represent the possibility of the future, the understanding of perfection, how perfect we could be."

What about the dogs? "Sometimes the dog plays the part of an antagonist or a predator. Or [it's] barking a warning." And the *X*s on his figures represented "either the location of or absence of heart and soul."

These were rare explanations. Usually, Keith listened to the subway riders, and then, without correcting or clarifying them, he smiled and handed them a button with an image of the crawling baby.

The drawings elicited responses besides curiosity, too.

A reader of *Time* magazine wrote: "Millions of passengers are oppressed, intimidated and degraded by these scribblings, which are not art but contemptuous vandalism."

Snarky passersby would ask Keith, "Don't you have anything better to do?" Or they would say that they were "really bored" with his work.

But negativity was the exception rather than the rule. Sometimes spectators would even erupt in applause as Keith finished a drawing.

"So many people wished me luck and told me to 'keep it up' that it became difficult to stop," he said.

It also became tough to keep up with demand, especially since the drawings would last only from a few hours to a few weeks. The constant turnover, along with his own drive to keep his drawings fresh, meant that Keith had to create a lot more images.

And that he did. Inspired by current events and pop culture, he drew dollar signs and crosses, computers and light bulbs, phones and pyramids, snakes and monkeys—anything he could use to attract the public's attention and share a message.

Drawing in the subway carried risks, of course. Although his works were G-rated and could easily be erased, writing on the panels was usually treated as vandalism—a criminal act, pure and simple.

Some transit police officers were fans. They would ask him for an autograph or a baby button. Or they would look the other way or take his chalk.

But other officers wouldn't hesitate to issue him a citation or even handcuff and arrest him.

"The worst thing that ever happened to me was being handcuffed and locked in a bathroom," Keith recalled, "and I was like scared to death the cop was gonna go chase a mugger or something and forget that I was in the bathroom, and I'd be just found there a skeleton with handcuffs on."

While he was no fan of being arrested, Keith never felt that the cops saw him as someone to rough up. "I'm white, I wear glasses, I don't look threatening," he explained, suggesting that the police tended to target Black and Brown people.

Was the chance of being hauled to jail worth it?

By 1985, when he stopped the subway project, Keith had amassed numerous police citations. He had also created about five thousand drawings for millions of everyday people.

Looking back on the subway project, Keith said: "I think in terms of what it represents and its pure philosophical statement, it is definitely the most important thing I have done."

What did that mean?

"The subway drawings were sort of my grand gesture to say fuck you to the art market," Keith explained.

They were a middle finger to the gallerists, dealers, and collectors who defined artworks primarily as commodities, as objects to be bought, sold, or traded.

They were a "fuck you" to the museum curators who sniffed at street art. To the artists who were obsessed with gaining wealthy clients. And to everyone who said fine art belonged only in museums, galleries, and the homes of wealthy patrons.

"Art was the symbol of the bourgeois and the people who could afford it and 'understand' it," he explained. "And it was used as a way of separating the general population from the upper class."

Rebelling against this history, Keith had taken his art directly to the masses and offered it freely, without charging a cent.

Art, after all, was for everybody.

What Do the Images Mean?

In 2018, the Albertina, a modern art museum in Vienna, Austria, had a special exhibit devoted to Keith's visual alphabet.

"Keith Haring's picture-word system was something like a predecessor to today's emojis," the museum said. As emojis embody meanings, so did Keith's cartoonish images.

The museum sought to unpack and explain its own interpretations of Keith's symbols. For example, it said that the **dog** "sometimes functions as a symbol of justice or embodies a protector, but it may also turn into a ravaging beast . . . that expresses the abuse of power."

The **flying saucer** symbolizes not just space and space travel but also "any person who lies outside of the social norm and community."

The **dollar sign** represents consumerism.

And **Mickey Mouse** "stands for Walt Disney and his studios, as well as for popular culture, capitalism, mass culture, and childhood."

ARE THE HUMAN FIGURES MALES?

In 1988, an interviewer asked Keith whether his human figures were men.

"No," he replied. "They don't have a race; they don't have an age; they don't have a sex. They are more signs for human, which in a way is saying that humans are basically all of the same quality and the same importance and that there doesn't have to be separation."

But Keith did make one exception. "If they have a pregnant stomach, they could be a woman because they have a pregnant stomach." But even pregnant figures lacked any other identifying characteristics, like female breasts.

6 DJ

DJ, 1983.

Keith was inspired by the DJs who spun the records at his favorite nightclubs. He played music wherever he worked and transferred his love of music and dance into art and art shows that challenged the staid, and primarily white, world of Manhattan's elite art galleries.

MUSIC

It was a typical night at the New St. Mark's Baths, the city's largest gay bathhouse, when a young man caught Keith's eye.

The two men cruised each other, and Keith was smitten. "I mean, he was Black, really thin, the same height as me . . . and he was almost the same age as me."

If Juan DuBose wasn't equally enamored, he was at least comfortable enough to share his phone number.

The next day, Keith called.

Juan didn't pick up.

Keith left a message and then just sat in the middle of his living room, staring at the phone, waiting and waiting.

Finally, it rang.

"It is Juan DuBose, and I fall madly and totally in love with him."

● ● ●

Juan lived with his sister in the Bronx, and although he worked in car stereo sales and repairs, his real passion was deejaying.

A month or so after the bathhouse encounter, Juan moved into a downtown loft that Keith shared with his close friend Samantha McEwen. Like Keith, Samantha was also impressed with Juan, finding him gentle, beautiful, and mysterious.

Juan DuBose and Keith in their New York City apartment, 1983.

Juan filled the apartment with the aromas of his cooking and the pulsating beats of dance music. He gave Keith countless mixtapes of the tracks featured in the city's Brown and Black clubs.

For years, Keith had blasted music when he worked. He had used a radio and a stereo in earlier times, but now he cranked up the volume on a boombox painted by Kenny Scharf.

"I work surrounded by music," Keith said.

Loud music, he might have added.

And lots of different types. In the mornings, he preferred relaxing music, like classical, jazz, tango, and reggae selections, and in the evening hours, he painted to the relentless beat of house music—anything danceable.

His well-worn mixtapes included Bach and Strauss, Aretha Franklin and Diana Ross, the B-52's and the Talking Heads, Prince and Madonna, the Beastie Boys and Yoko Ono—and many, many more.

By Keith's own account, music affected his mood and influenced his art.

"Music in New York is part of daily life, it's everywhere," he said. "And for me . . . it makes you feel good, it inspires you, it uplifts you. For me this is art's role."

Subway drawing of a pink boombox dancer, 1984.

That's what Keith saw as the role of *his* art, too—to delight, inspire, and uplift. So, with music bouncing off his studio walls, he channeled his own good feelings into creating images that would make people smile.

Radiant babies and barking dogs.

Red hearts and blue bunnies.

Singing dolphins and winged mermaids.

Bikini-wearing pigs and crazy caterpillars.

And that crazy three-eyed face!

Music also affected the *process* of Keith's artmaking.

"To me music is really important while I'm working to keep the rhythm and keep the pace of the painting," he explained.

Art curator Jeffrey Deitch says that Keith's process was like that of "a great saxophonist and a jazz solo. He would start in the upper-left corner of a wall or a canvas, and move across in perfect rhythm, never missing a beat. Other artists had to make a sketch or use a grid system to cover the canvas."

But Keith didn't typically use sketches or grids. "He had this remarkable ability to transfer the images that he saw in his mind through his body, through his hand, and onto the surface."

The indispensable tool that made this transfer so easy, so effortless, was Keith's beloved music—the mixtapes that kept everything flowing in the right direction.

And then there was dancing.

On most Saturday nights, Keith and Juan would walk up the ramp inside the Paradise Garage, an old parking garage converted into a nightclub.

It was "gay night," and most of the people in line were Black and Brown men. This was no glitzy disco crowd. Glittery silk shirts and white bell-bottoms were out—tight shorts, T-shirts, and sneakers were in.

Keith and Juan felt the bass from the club's powerful sound system reverberating in their chests as they made their way up the long ramp.

Inside, the couple strolled past makeshift seats covered with gray carpet and then headed to the massive dance floor. A shiny disco ball hung from the ceiling, lights flashed across the room, and more than a thousand people grooved to the beats.

"Everyone was there to dance, to sweat, to listen to the music, and to be quite honest with you, to get high," says Garage patron Kat Ayala.

Keith's pale skin and round glasses made him stand out—so did his dancing. "He moved in his own way," friend Benny Soto recalls. "It was definitely odd, very weird. But that was attractive to me—it was different."

Keith dancing beneath his art at the Paradise Garage, 1987.

After a few dances, Juan took off for his favorite place—the booth where the DJ Larry Levan spun the records. Levan's tastes were eclectic, with an emphasis on funk and garage music, and he was known for creating his own house dance tracks. Partiers had no choice but to go with his flow, and they did so with utter abandon.

Keith was so enthralled by the Garage that he spent most Saturday nights there, and not for just a few hours, either; a trip to the Garage would typically last from seven to ten hours.

The chance to vibe with the crowd was reason enough to clear his schedule. "But it was more than that," Benny says. "Keith felt acceptance there. He didn't feel judged. And that's what we all want, right? A place that accepts us, where we fit in, where we belong."

There was another reason for Keith's devotion to the Garage. He quickly discovered that the rapturous dancing, like the music in his studio, influenced and shaped his artwork.

While dancing, he thought of new art projects and took mental images of the dancers around him so he could later transfer them to his drawings and paintings.

Like those new phenoms on the scene—breakdancers.

• • •

Rich "Crazy Legs" Colón, the leader of the Rock Steady Crew, the best-known breaking crew in New York City, lunged a few steps forward.

Then he sprang backward and sideways, darting to the left and right, before dropping to the floor. With his legs soaring high above the ground, he executed a roll from his back to his front, shifting effortlessly from shoulder to shoulder in a dizzying display of skill and dexterity. He called it "the windmill."

Keith was a huge fan.

He probably first saw the Rock Steady Crew at Negril or the Roxy, two of downtown New York's first hip-hop clubs. He also caught them at the Kitchen, an art collective, and at a party hosted by graffiti artists Fab 5 Freddy and Futura.

"One day Futura and I gave a party at our studio and the Rock Steady Crew came," Fab recalls. "We had no music. And Keith came, and I think Kenny [Scharf] was there, and we all just clapped our hands, and the Rock Steady Crew started dancing."

Keith was no breakdancer, but he was moved.

"Breakdancing was a real inspiration, seeing the kids spinning and twisting around on their heads," he said. "So my drawings began having figures spinning on their heads and twisting around."

● ● ●

Keith painting the mural at Houston Street and Bowery, New York City, 1982.

In the summer of 1982, Keith and Juan headed to a freestanding concrete wall at the corner of Houston Street and Bowery in the Lower East Side. The wall was surrounded by piles of smelly trash.

After filling dozens of garbage bags, Keith and Juan painted the wall with fluorescent Day-Glo white. Keith then created a mural showing four large human figures dancing on their heads.

To anyone familiar with New York's club scenes and street life, the green figures were instantly recognizable as the young dancers populating the clubs and streets.

Breakdancers also appeared in numerous paintings Keith made at the time.

While he was drawing in the subway, Keith continued to make conventional paintings in his studio. The New York art world took notice, and buyers began to offer large sums of money for his works.

Although Keith appreciated the attention and money, he did not like conducting business, so Tony Shafrazi, an up-and-coming gallerist, served as his art dealer. In October 1982, the Tony Shafrazi Gallery hosted Keith's first major art show, which included his collaborations with a young graffiti artist named LA II (see chapter 10).

"I guess I wasn't so 'radical' that I wanted to totally abandon the art world," Keith recalled about his willingness to have a gallery show.

At the show's opening, breakdancers, rappers, and graffiti artists mixed with classical music lovers and patrons of so-called high art. Even children were present, coloring in books that Keith had designed for the occasion. The event had a hip-hop and Garage-esque feel. Guests saw images of breakers on a narrow white strip that ran from the floor to the ceiling, as well as a line of breakers running parallel to the floor. Downstairs, they would see Juan DuBose spinning dance music in a room basked in black light.

The show was a critical and commercial success, and Keith was now a rising star in the New York art world, and beyond.

Back at the Garage—he was always back at the Garage—Keith saw another new dance gaining in popularity.

The electric boogie.

Like breaking, it was extraordinarily difficult. The few who could master it moved their bodies as if electric jolts were passing through them. The dance might start with a jerking arm, but by the end, the dancer's entire body would be vibrating with energy. Sometimes, a dancer would use their fingers or hands to pass electric currents from their body to the bodies of other dancers, all of them eventually jerking and twitching this way and that.

Keith was no electric boogier, but he was electrified.

In the subway, he drew a dancing figure's arms and legs emitting so much energy that they powered a light bulb that served as the figure's head. Another

picture showed an electric boogier powering their boombox head. And still another showed a dancer whose entire body resembled an electric jolt.

As penises had appeared in Keith's art when he came out as a gay man, breakdancers and electric boogiers were now exploding through his chalk, pens, and paintbrushes. At one and the same time, they were a celebration of urban dance and an expression of Keith's overall goal of uplifting people and making them feel good.

Although he visited other clubs, Paradise Garage remained Keith's favorite.

Years later, he described his time at the Garage as an echo of his early days of following the Grateful Dead. "The whole experience was very communal, very spiritual."

By the time the Garage closed in 1987, Keith had long been its unofficial resident artist. He had painted its walls and created art for special events, like the "Rain Dance" benefit to combat hunger in Africa.

After dancing the night away on the club's final night, he went home and wrote that the closing felt like "losing a lover when everything was going just fine."

Of course, music and dance did not disappear from Keith's life. He moved on to other music and other dance clubs, and both art forms continued to exert remarkable influence over his art.

Keith created posters for the Montreux Jazz Festival; a famous mural with lyrics from Public Enemy's rap song "Don't Believe the Hype"; public sculptures of dancing figures; album covers for David Bowie, Run DMC, and other musician-friends; and so much more.

Perhaps his most famous cover was for *A Very Special Christmas*, a 1987 album that raised more than $160 million for the Special Olympics. The cover was another example of Keith's ongoing commitment to artistic projects that benefited social causes near and dear to his heart.

7 AGAINST NUKES

UNTITLED, 1982.

ONE OF MANY PAINTINGS AND POSTERS OPPOSING NUCLEAR WEAPONS AND CELEBRATING PEACE AND LOVE. KEITH MADE ART THAT EXPRESSED HIS OPINIONS ABOUT POLITICS AND SOCIAL ISSUES.

PROTEST

IT WAS A CLOUDY SPRING DAY, WITH TEMPERATURES IN THE 60S, as hundreds of thousands of people descended on Central Park. They were on a mission—to rally against nuclear weapons and war.

At the time, the United States and the Soviet Union were opposed in the Cold War, a clash that pitted capitalist countries against communist ones. To win the so-called war—which rarely saw open conflict—the two countries spent billions of dollars for nuclear weapons designed to wipe each other from the face of the earth.

"No nukes!" shouted the demonstrators.

A little girl held a sign that summed up the day's protest: "I Hate Nuclear War."

Keith, too, was on a mission—to hand out posters he had created for the protest.

Handing out his free anti-nuclear posters,
New York City, 1982.

There was nothing playful about them. They were produced in black and white rather than in the vibrant Day-Glo colors he was known for, and their content was sobering.

The top half of the poster showed a cloud caused by a nuclear explosion, and in the middle of the cloud was an innocent victim—the crawling baby. Three angels flew above the baby and the bomb.

The poster that Keith gave away at the 1982 anti-nuclear rally.

The meaning of Keith's art was not always clear, but this one was hard to miss.

Keith had paid for twenty thousand posters, and now he and his friends stood outside Central Park, rolling them up and handing them out as fast as possible.

Their pace was so frantic that by the end of the day, they had given away fourteen thousand, hoping that people would hang them in homes, schools, workplaces, and bars—all the places that would be zapped to smithereens in the event of a nuclear explosion.

Meanwhile, rally speaker Helen Caldicott, a pediatrician and president of Physicians for Social Responsibility, denounced nuclear weapons. "We're thinking of our babies," she said. "There are no Communist babies; there are no capitalist babies. A baby is a baby is a baby!"

Keith disagreed not only with then-president Ronald Reagan's massive buildup of nuclear weapons, but also with the use of religion to justify pro-nuclear policies.

Reverend Jerry Falwell, a conservative Baptist minister and fervent Reagan supporter, used his popular TV and radio shows to claim that the Soviet Union was a godless country, and that if it won the arms race, it would overrun the United States and abolish precious freedoms, such as the freedom to worship.

Falwell's message—which echoed the president's own words—riled Keith so much that he made a subway drawing about it.

Using his typical bold lines, Keith drew a menacing figure with the head of a wolf. Just beyond the wolf's vicious snout was a talking bubble in the shape of a cloud with a nuclear symbol inside. In one hand, the pro-nuclear wolf held a leash that restrained a crawling human figure, and in the other, it raised a Christian cross.

Anyone paying attention to the news would have interpreted the wolf as a symbol of either man, or of any leader who used religion to support nuclear weapons.

Two years later, on September 26, 1984, while Reagan was running for his second term, Keith was back in the subway, making more anti-nuclear drawings.

"Another drawing today was this guy with a TV head, waving an American flag," he told an interviewer. "He has a cross in his hand. In the other hand, he has missiles. He was stepping on all these people. . . . And on his chest it said 'Ronald Reagan, '84.'"

Keith fully understood that the drawing was provocative and that its anti-Reagan message was obvious.

"I guess it was so obvious that by the time I got back to the other side—I went uptown, turned around and came back downtown—[the] drawing had been destroyed already. Some Reagan person, I'm sure, was offended by it, and ripped it up."

This wasn't the first time that Keith's anti-Reagan work was destroyed.

In August 1980, when Reagan was running for his first term as president, Keith had jumped on his bike and wheat-pasted anti-Reagan posters on light poles and newsstands across Manhattan.

"Some people were infuriated by them and would scratch them or rip them off," Keith recalled. "It's fun when you're putting them up and people get outraged and try to peel them off while they're still wet, because then they get wheat paste all over their hands, and they get even madder."

One of Keith's boldest acts for peace occurred in 1986, when a human rights group asked him to paint the western side of the Berlin Wall—an ugly cement wall, topped with barbed wire, that divided West Germany from East Germany.

Built by East Berlin in 1961, partly to keep its citizens from fleeing to the West, the fourteen-foot-high wall symbolized the Cold War and the ongoing division between the capitalist West and the communist East.

Keith knew that he would not be the first artist to paint on the wall, but he still found the invitation exciting.

Like drawing in the subway, painting the Wall would allow him to reach masses of people who did not typically visit art galleries and museums. Equally attractive, it would be a creative and nonviolent way to agitate for peace.

On the morning of October 3, 1986, Keith headed to the Berlin Wall.

The six feet of land in front of the Wall's entire western side was East German territory, so getting close enough to paint required entering the communist country.

Keith did not have a travel visa that would have allowed him to visit East Germany legally, but he did not seem overly concerned as he cranked his boombox, grabbed his brush, and began to paint.

That illegal act prompted a West Berlin police officer to inform Keith that he was in East Germany without a visa and defacing property.

Not one to be deterred by mere laws, Keith painted on. But he did keep an eye on the East German border troops, and whenever he thought they might be about to arrest him, he would jump back into West German territory.

"They had binoculars trained on me, cameras clicking practically the whole time, and then their heads appeared over the top of the wall to glare at me at point-blank range," he said later. "I tell you, it was a bit scary."

Keith painting the Berlin Wall, 1986.

• • •

While hundreds of West Berliners gathered, Keith painted red and black human figures on a yellow background. The colors were deliberately chosen; all three were part of both countries' flags.

Keith connected the figures in a long chain. The hands of a red figure held onto the legs of a black figure, the hands of a black figure held on to the feet of a red figure, and on it went.

Journalists asked him what it all meant. Although he rarely answered questions about the meaning of his work, this time Keith made an exception.

"The human chain was painted red and black because those colors belong to both parts of Germany and are to symbolize a mutual exchange between both sides of the Wall," he said.

When someone suggested that the mural seemed to target only East Germany, Keith balked. "It's for people and it doesn't matter which side of the wall they're on," he said. "It's about both sides coming together."

Perhaps most significantly, he described the mural as "a political and subversive act—an attempt to psychologically destroy the wall by painting it."

But Keith also saw his mural as an attempt to destroy other barriers to peace and unity, not merely the one between East and West Germans. "For me the Berlin Wall is the most symbolic wall that one can paint," he said. "It is a metaphor for other walls that exist in the mind—for instance, in South Africa, Nicaragua, and Belfast."

Two years later, in July 1988, Keith and a group of friends visited another symbolic site—Hiroshima, Japan.

On August 6, 1945, near the end of World War II, the United States dropped an atomic bomb on the city, razing its buildings and killing 140,000 people. The heat from the bomb was so intense that some people simply vanished.

After the war, Hiroshima built museums and parks to remind the public of the horrors of the atomic bomb.

Keith's trip to the city included a visit to the Hiroshima Peace Memorial Museum, which uses photographs, videos, and historic relics, like burned student uniforms, to educate the public about the destruction.

"It is impossible to imagine the magnitude of the bombing until you personally experience this museum," Keith wrote in his journal.

"There was one photo of human skulls that was beyond reality. Pictures of radioactivity's aftereffects were nothing short of science-fiction horror. Descriptions of black rain drops, photos of melted faces, etc., etc."

Part of the museum's collection included photos of President Jimmy Carter and his teenage daughter, Amy, visiting the site in 1984. An image of Amy deeply affected Keith.

"In one picture all you can see is one eye and part of her head, since she is standing behind her father. The terror in her eye is so real and so sincere that it riveted me to tears."

After touring the museum, Keith and his friends walked through Peace Memorial Park in silence. "It was not necessary to speak, for everyone understood," he noted.

The group then met with local leaders, and Keith made plans to paint a mural at an elementary school that faced Peace Memorial Park. Perhaps most enjoyable was visiting a local gallery.

While there I met this 76-year-old mother (a survivor of Hiroshima), who was my big fan. I did a big drawing for her, much to her delight.

WORLD PEACE

In June 1989, Keith painted *Tuttomondo*, a mural on the rectory, or parish house, of Sant'Antonio Church in Pisa, Italy. It was one of his last major public projects, and he hoped it would exist for hundreds of years. Its message, he said, was about "harmony," "unity," and "the world at peace."

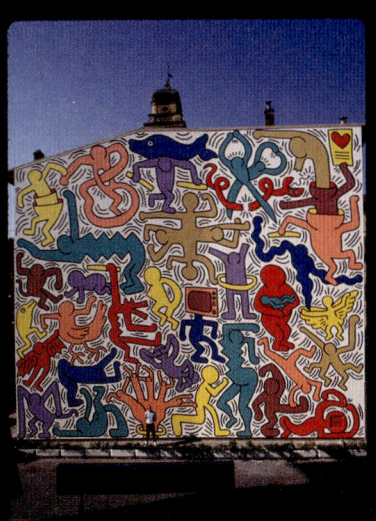

Keith in front of the *Tuttomondo* mural in Pisa, Italy, 1989.

8 MICHAEL STEWART— USA FOR AFRICA

MICHAEL STEWART—USA FOR AFRICA, 1985.

This painting expresses Keith's anger and revulsion at the police killing of Black artist Michael Stewart in New York in 1985. Keith made anti-racist drawings and paintings that criticized government-sanctioned brutality against Black and Brown people.

RACE AND RETRIBUTION

KEITH AND JUAN DUBOSE WERE RENOWNED FOR THROWING fabulous parties at their Broome Street apartment in Lower Manhattan. Juan spun the dance tunes, Keith drew, and friends danced and chilled—at least until John Sex wandered in with his boa constrictor.

"The whole downtown crowd would be there," remembers Paige Powell, Andy Warhol's assistant and friend.

Congregating in the kitchen, some of the guests, like Fred "Fab 5 Freddy" Brathwaite and Rich "Crazy Legs" Colón, tagged the white refrigerator door. An ambitious young singer added, "Madonna Loves Keith."

On the night of September 14, 1983, Michael Stewart, a 25-year-old Black artist, showed up for one of the parties. He was accompanied by painter George Condo and a third person with whom Keith had had a disagreement.

When Keith saw the third person, he made up an excuse not to let them in. The party was getting out of hand, he said.

The tagged refrigerator door from Keith and Juan DuBose's apartment.

So the three left, and Michael moved on to the nearby Pyramid Club, a favorite hangout for artistic and gender-fluid clubbers.

Not long before 3:00 a.m., while waiting to take the train back home to Brooklyn, Michael tagged a subway wall.

The transit police spotted him, a chase ensued, and Michael ended up on the ground, where officers, according to eyewitnesses, handcuffed and beat him. The police later denied the beating, claiming they had simply restrained him after he resisted arrest.

By the time the officers transported Michael to Bellevue Hospital, he had suffered cardiac arrest and slipped into a coma.

The following night, artist Jean-Michel Basquiat told Keith that the cops had almost killed Michael.

Keith had first met Jean-Michel when he was still a student at the School of Visual Arts. Jean-Michel—who was not a student—had asked for help with entering the school's secure building, and Keith had been all too happy to lend a hand.

At the end of the day, Keith noticed that the school had been spraypainted with numerous antiestablishment sayings tagged by SAMO©, a famous, anonymous, and prolific artist whose literary graffiti appeared throughout Lower Manhattan.

It didn't take long for Keith to figure out that the young Black man he had let into the building was SAMO©. (More exactly, Jean-Michel was one-half of the tag; the other half was his cohort, Al Diaz.)

Keith was a huge fan of Jean-Michel's work, and the two eventually bonded over their appreciation for each other's art. At the time of Michael Stewart's beating, Keith and Jean-Michel were rising stars in the international art world.

"He was completely freaked out," Keith said of Jean-Michel's reaction to the news about Michael Stewart. "It was like it could have been him."

Keith was rattled, too, since he had not let Michael into his apartment and the fateful night could have had a much different ending.

The downtown arts scene galvanized around Michael, and leaders organized a protest in Union Square for September 26. To help advertise the protest, artist David Wojnarowicz designed a haunting poster that showed two police officers, with white skulls for heads, brutalizing a handcuffed and bloodied Black man.

Two days after the protest, Michael died.

Reverend Ben Chavis—who would later head the National Association for the Advancement of Colored People—told the *New York Times* that

Jean-Michel-Basquiat (center) with Keith (right) and John McLaughlin (John Sex, left) at Area nightclub, 1984.

"the unfortunate death of Michael Stewart should bring everybody back to the real issue: too many black, Hispanic and other minorities being victims of unmitigated [police] violence."

Shortly after Michael's death, Keith vented in Andy Warhol's studio. "Keith was ranting and raving about this black graffiti artist that's in the papers now because the police killed him—Michael Stewart," Warhol said. "And Keith said that he's been arrested by the police four times, but that because he looks normal they just sort of call him a fairy and let him go. But this kid that was killed, he had the Jean-Michel look—dreadlocks."

Sometime later, Jean-Michel showed up at Keith's studio, found a spot on the wall, and painted a picture of two large police officers, one with sharp teeth, both with red faces, using their batons to beat a smaller Black man who stood between them.

"It could have been me," Jean-Michel kept saying.

Artist Suzanne Mallouk, Jean-Michel's former partner, had dated Michael, and she played a leading role in organizing the Michael Stewart Justice Committee, a volunteer group that hired lawyers to win justice for Michael and his family in the courts.

"I hired his legal team, raising money from the arts community," she recalls. "I went to every gallery that was showing graffiti art and asked for donations."

Suzanne also approached individual artists, including Keith, who sold a painting to support the cause.

In September 1985, six white transit police officers finally went on trial for charges related to Michael's death.

The officers' attorneys claimed that Michael had been drunk, that he injured himself when resisting arrest, and that he died of a heart attack. Prosecuting attorneys said that the officers had brutalized Michael and that he died of strangulation, perhaps from a chokehold.

In October, Keith painted a gruesome image of a naked Black man strangled by two white arms holding a crooked rod. The victim's right hand was handcuffed to a white skeleton holding a key, and his left hand was cuffed to a snake eating a peace dove.

Surrounding the man—who was screaming silently—were three yellow human figures covering their eyes and mouth, deliberately refusing to look at the violence unfolding before them.

The content was raw, visceral, gut-wrenching—unlike the lighthearted art that Keith was known for.

A month later, all six officers were acquitted. Even New York City Mayor Ed Koch, who was not known for siding against the police, was concerned enough to urge the city's Metropolitan Transportation Authority (MTA) to investigate Michael's death further.

Two years later, the MTA board decided not to charge the officers with using excessive force. Keith unloaded in his journal:

Today I read in the New York Times that all of the officers who killed Michael Stewart were again dismissed of charges.

Continually dismissed, but in their minds they will not forget. They know they killed him. They will never forget his screams, his face, his blood. They must live with that forever.

I hope in their next life they are tortured like they tortured him. . . .

An eye for an eye.

Although Keith often celebrated peace and love in his work, he certainly did not draw from those values when considering the fate of the transit officers. In 1988, when asked if he believed in turning the other cheek, he said: "Yes, to a degree. I also believe in an eye for an eye. . . . It would be great if people are going to get theirs later on."

In the mid-1980s, hundreds of thousands of people across the United States demonstrated against racial apartheid in South Africa.

For decades, the white minority who controlled the country had jailed leading Black dissidents, including Nelson Mandela, and tortured and killed Black people for protesting for their rights. In 1976, for instance, a clash between white police officers and Black students protesting a government decree that required certain subjects to be taught in Afrikaans, the language spoken by the white minority, resulted in the killing of more than five hundred Black people.

Keith supported the anti-apartheid protests by creating a special poster. Produced in red and black, it showed an image of a large Black human figure with a leash around its neck, trampling on a white human figure who was holding but also losing control of the leash: a depiction of South Africa's Black majority revolting against the white minority who enforced apartheid. To drive home his message, Keith added bold-faced words to the bottom of the poster—"Free South Africa."

Keith paid for twenty thousand copies of the anti-apartheid poster, and at one protest in 1985, he got on his knees, rolled up copies of the poster, and handed them out, free of charge, just as he had done with his anti-nuclear

FREE SOUTH AFRICA

Keith turned this 1985 painting into 20,000 posters.

Keith handing out *Free South Africa* posters, New York City, 1985.

poster a few years earlier. Keith and his friends eventually gave away all, or almost all, of the posters.

"Most white men are evil," Keith wrote in his journal. "All stories of white men's 'expansion' and 'colonization' and 'domination' are filled with horrific details of the abuse of power and the misuse of people."

Physically, Keith was about as white as a person could be, but when he looked within himself, he did not see the whiteness associated with colonialism and racism. "I'm sure inside I'm not white," he wrote.

In a later interview, he added: "Maybe I was black in another life or something."

Keith also reflected on race in his thoughts about his partner, Juan DuBose.

"I'm terrifically comfortable with Juan," he said. "But then, I'm always more comfortable with people of color—much more than white people. It isn't something I specifically look for, but from the time I was a little kid, I had this tremendous guilt about what white people have done to people of color."

By the end of 1985, Keith and Juan had broken up. It's not clear what Juan thought of the split, but Keith said he started to pull away because Juan wasn't applying himself to constructive projects.

In January 1986, while dancing at the Paradise Garage, Keith found himself deeply attracted to another young man. "I look at him and see that he's the man of my dreams," Keith said.

He was Juan Rivera—a 28-year-old Puerto Rican, jobless at this point, but a former house painter, construction worker, and sex worker.

Juan knew a bit about Keith at the time of their meeting. "I was familiar with his subway art, but didn't think it was all *that*," he said. "'Cause I thought any caveman could've done it."

But Juan's perspective changed the moment he saw Keith painting in the studio. "When I saw him *doing* it—Jesus Christ!—it was amazing! I mean, the energy just flowed through him."

Several months after hooking up, Juan and Keith moved into a new apartment and created a life together. "I cooked and kept the house clean," Juan said.

After dinner, the two would often kick back, smoke pot, and watch TV, usually *Mister Ed*, *The Honeymooners*, and, of course, cartoons.

● ● ●

Living with Keith wasn't always easy for Juan, especially since Keith loved playing host to lots of young Brown and Black men in his studio.

"I knew that was part of his creative energy—what made his energy flow—'cause there would always be a bunch of kids hanging out at his studio watching him paint, and he'd always have great music, food from *Balducci's* [a gourmet grocery store], and the *best* pot. And it was cool, *real* cool watching him paint . . . but *damn*!!" Juan said.

At various points, he discovered that Keith was also having sex with other men. According to Juan, when he confronted Keith, "He'd make it sound like, 'Juan, don't worry! I'm always gonna take care of you. That's just the way I am.' So I said, Okay . . . But I always knew there would eventually be someone else."

Was Keith Racist?

Many of the artists who pioneered graffiti and street art were people of color. Did Keith appropriate these and other elements of Black and Brown culture—breakdancing, for example—for his own gain and without giving credit?

Scholar Ricardo Montez thinks so, and he has taken issue with Keith's claim that inside he was not white.

"He's really trying to distance himself from this history of white oppression and violence," Montez says. "But Keith was steeped in whiteness, and exactly because he was white, he benefitted from the past and present system of white racism."

Montez says that it was problematic for Keith to believe that he could grasp what it meant to be a Black or Brown person. As Montez puts this, "[Keith] says that his spirit and soul are much closer to people of color. So there is a fantasy he has, where he thinks he can access this kind of thing. It's racist. It's a kind of white liberal fantasy that you can know the difference of the other that you want to take from, to be."

On the other hand, Keith provided opportunities for some artists of color. He brought the Black and Brown graffiti scene into mainstream galleries, curated exhibitions with Black and Brown artists, and gave graffiti writer LA II (see chapter 10) the chance to travel and sell his art.

9 ANDY MOUSE

ANDY MOUSE, 1986.

ANDY WARHOL, MICKEY MOUSE, AND THE DOLLAR BILL: THREE RECOGNIZABLE IMAGES FROM U.S. POP CULTURE. A NEO- ("NEW") POP ARTIST, KEITH TOOK ITEMS FROM EVERYDAY LIFE AND MADE THEM INTO FINE ART. HE OPENED A RETAIL STORE, TOO, THAT MADE HIS POPULAR ART AVAILABLE TO A WIDER AUDIENCE—A SUBVERSION OF THE ESTABLISHED ART WORLD'S ATTEMPTS TO CONTROL THE PRODUCTION AND DISTRIBUTION OF FINE ART.

MONEY AND FAME

THE SUBWAY DRAWINGS GROUND TO A HALT IN LATE 1985.

"These drawings had run their course, because they had achieved what I wanted them to achieve and that was getting the work out to the public at large," Keith explained.

There was another reason, too. "Word had gotten out that my prices were rising more and more, and people just cut the drawings out of their panels and sold them."

But Keith wanted to continue reaching people who did not typically visit art museums and galleries, so he came up with another radical idea—a retail store with affordable art.

On April 19, 1986, Keith opened the Pop Shop on Lafayette Street in Lower Manhattan.

The shop itself was a work of art. Keith had painted its interior walls, floors, and ceilings, and the merchandise was artfully displayed on walls and shelves.

Many of the colorful products showcased Keith's crawling babies, barking dogs, and breakdancers.

Items included T-shirts and sweatshirts, radios and watches, pins and charms, and posters and buttons, with prices ranging from fifty cents for the buttons to $350 for a jacket. Inflatable babies, packaged in a small white box, cost twelve dollars.

Keith saw the entire enterprise as "an art statement." Yes, some of the items were cheap, but "we didn't want to produce things that would cheapen the art," he said. That meant no coffee mugs, pens, and shower curtains—things he considered kitschy.

Keith carrying Zena Scharf in front of an advertisement for the Pop Shop, New York City, 1987.

When the critics sniped anyway, accusing him of crass commercialism, Keith snapped back. "If commercialization is putting my art on a shirt so that a kid who can't afford a $30,000 painting can buy one, then I'm all for it. Art is nothing if you don't reach every segment of the people."

And when someone spraypainted "Capitalist" at the store's entrance, Keith defended himself by saying that artistic and commercial success can go hand in hand.

More to the point, he insisted that the primary purpose of the store was not to turn a profit but to make art accessible to the wider public. The Pop Shop was for the people, not for Keith's bank account.

"Ultimately, I don't care about what critics say," Keith added. "I'm more interested in what real people think."

The shop never generated a huge income, but under the management of Keith's friend Bobby Breslau, the shop sometimes experienced financial stability, with profits going to AIDS organizations and educational programs for children.

"I wanna be pop!" Keith announced around the time of the store's opening.

This wasn't exactly an aspirational statement, or a dream, because Keith already considered his work as "pop," or more exactly, as part of the legacy of the Pop art movement.

Historically, "Pop" artists were known for elevating parts of mass media and popular culture into works of fine art. Rebelling against abstract art, Pop artists made vibrantly colored pieces that reflected and represented the lives and interests of everyday people.

Begun in the 1950s, Pop art hit its peak in the 1960s, when Andy Warhol, often referred to as the King of Pop, skyrocketed to fame with his paintings of Campbell soup cans and his silk-screened images of celebrities such as Marilyn Monroe, Jacqueline Kennedy, and Elvis.

Keith wasn't part of the first Pop wave, of course, but he eventually became known as a leading figure in the "Neo-Pop" movement begun in the 1980s—though, for the record, Keith insisted that "there's not really a word that describes easily the kind of work I do."

As a fan of Pop art, Keith adored Andy Warhol.

Andy Warhol and Keith at the Limelight nightclub, 1984.

When he was still a student at the School of Visual Arts, Keith spotted the famous artist inside a coffeeshop near the Museum of Modern Art.

Nervous and excited, he paced back and forth in front of the building.

What should I do? he wondered.

Should I go in?

Stealing several more glimpses, Keith agonized about what he would say if he did go in.

But then he chickened out and left.

More inner torture occurred when he attended an opening for one of Andy's exhibitions in 1979. As usual, Andy armed himself against the fawning masses by holding copies of *Interview* magazine close to his chest and handing them out to admirers.

"He gave me a copy, but again I was totally speechless," Keith said. "I didn't know what to say."

Finally, in 1983, after Andy had stopped by an exhibit of hip hop-themed works by Keith and collaborator LA II at the Fun Gallery, the two artists spoke one-on-one.

A mutual friend, photographer Christopher Makos, introduced them, and a friendship quickly bloomed. Keith visited Andy's infamous studio, the Factory, and Andy hung out at Keith's parties on Broome Street. Along the way, the two exchanged art and collaborated on a few pieces.

In August 1983, Andy invited Keith and Juan DuBose to stop by the Factory so he could take their photos and turn them into silk-screened portraits. Sitting in front of the camera, the couple stripped off their shirts and embraced each other.

"They were so lovey-dovey in the photos, it was nutty to see," Andy said.

The final portrait, produced mostly in orange, probably to suggest romantic heat, showed Juan sitting behind Keith and holding him gently. The couple loved it and hung it in their living room.

That's where Madonna saw it.

Keith had met Madonna long before she became a famous pop singer.

Perhaps they bumped into each other at the Roxy, where both enjoyed the hip-hop scene. Or maybe at the Fun House, a largely Latinx club where

Madonna dances at Keith's "Party of Life" at the Paradise Garage, 1984. Her pink leather suit was made by Hector Torres and painted by Keith and LA II.

Madonna danced to the tunes spun by her boyfriend, "Jellybean" Benitez, and performed some of her earliest songs.

"I don't know *what* drew [me and Keith] to these exotic clubs—like the Fun House or Paradise Garage," Madonna said. "Obviously, it was the sexuality and the animal-like magnetism of those people getting up and dancing with such abandon! They were all so beautiful!"

Madonna and Keith became close friends, hanging out in each other's apartments and in Keith's studio. One day, she swung by the studio and played him songs from her forthcoming album, *Like a Virgin*. Keith asked her to debut two of the songs, "Dress You Up" and "Like a Virgin," at his upcoming "Party of Life" at the Paradise Garage.

On the day of the party, May 16, 1984, Madonna performed before a crowd of three thousand, including Andy Warhol and a handful of other celebrities. For "Dress You Up," she wore a pink leather skirt showing Keith's artwork, and for "Like a Virgin," she writhed in lacy clothes on a big brass bed.

Four months later, Madonna would sing "Like a Virgin" on the first annual MTV Video Music Awards show. It was her biggest gig yet, and a foretaste of even greater fame.

As Madonna and Keith grew in popularity, both encountered artists who accused them of selling out—of becoming pop at the expense of artistic integrity and purity. "Of course, it's what *they* want too!" Madonna said of their critics. She added:

It's so transparent! They're just filled with jealousy and envy. And it certainly didn't stop us, because Keith didn't want to do his work just for the people of New York City—he wanted to do it for everybody, everywhere. I mean, an artist wants world recognition! He wants to make an impression on the world. He doesn't just want a small, sophisticated, elitist group of people appreciating his work.

By 1985, Madonna was well on her way to world recognition. "Like a Virgin" had hit No. 1 on the Billboard Hot 100 chart, and "Material Girl" was nominated for best female video at the second annual MTV awards.

Keith couldn't keep up with his friend's lightning-quick ascendence, and it seems he was rather envious of all the media attention she received. Perhaps no one understood this better than Andy Warhol, a veteran publicity hound.

When Andy and Keith arrived for the 1985 MTV awards show, Keith's desperate craving for attention became a bit too much even for Andy.

"Keith just wanted to be photographed so badly," Andy recalled. "And he wanted to go with me so he'd be sure to be photographed. So we got to Radio

City and it was just the biggest mob there, but the TV cameras had already left so Keith was really upset."

Andy found his sidekick even more insufferable when they joined a group of friends for a post-show dinner at the Odeon, a fancy French restaurant.

"Keith wanted to go right to the [nightclub] Palladium because he didn't want to miss the stars," Andy wrote. "So we got to the Odeon and he was immediately wanting to leave. . . . I mean, I like Keith, but it was so sick."

Although Keith was not in the stratosphere of celebrities like Madonna, his appeal landed him on TV shows and in popular magazines like *People*, *Newsweek,* and *Time*.

How did respected art critics and museum curators respond?

"Keith Haring's work is obviously very seductive and immensely attractive to a lot of people," said Michael Brenson, an art critic with the *New York Times*. "But there never seems to be any edge to it. . . . I don't care for it at all."

Newsweek art critic Mark Stevens agreed, deriding Haring's art as "fast food." "It's a good time," Stevens said. "It's boogeying on Saturday night. But great—no."

Suzanne Muchnic, of the *Los Angeles Times*, defended Haring's work but also agreed with the purists "who correctly point out that Haring's art is thin and repetitive—the sort of stuff that's made for reproduction—and that his conception of the human form never matures beyond cartoons and cookie cutters."

Andy Warhol faced similar criticism, and he was disturbed by the barbs shot in Keith's direction. He was also upset that museum curators, particularly the Museum of Modern Art (MoMA) in New York City, largely ignored Keith's works—and his own.

"Keith Haring isn't at MoMA," Andy lamented in his diary. "And they have just *one* thing of mine, the little Marilyn. I just hate that. That bothers me."

On February 22, 1987, after routine gall bladder surgery, Andy Warhol died from cardiac arrest. His untimely death surprised the public and rocked the art world.

Keith penned a tribute to his friend in his journal, calling Andy "the most important artist since Picasso."

He also noted that Andy's Pop art had not earned him a lot of respect from the art establishment.

"The museum and auction worlds didn't know how to deal with him."

Later that year, Keith complained that museums ignored his work, too. The issue came to the fore when a girl asked him to sign a poster of his work that she had purchased at the Tate, an art museum in London.

"It's really funny to me how all these museums sell poster and postcard reproductions of my art, but refuse to exhibit, collect or even acknowledge it within the museum," Keith wrote in his journal. "They want to play with me, but they don't have the balls to stand up and support me now."

But even as he grumbled about museums not displaying his works, Keith also sounded a rebellious note. "I should be glad, I suppose, that I am still outside of their acceptance. It gives me a freedom and gives me something to work against."

Ignored by museums, Keith felt free to pursue what he called "pure art."

Keith in his Manhattan studio, 1983.

As he explained this, "The only time [art] remains pure is when you are doing it at a real public level without monetary compensation or when you do it totally for yourself in seclusion."

For an example, Keith turned to public works involving children. "When I do drawings with or for children, there is a level of sincerity that seems honest and pure."

Anyone who knew him would not have been surprised by that statement. Keith loved kids.

10 DANCING FEMALES

UNTITLED, 1983.

PREGNANT FIGURES DANCING, AND A RADIANT BABY FLOATING: KEITH ADORED CHILDREN AND DREAMED OF BECOMING A FATHER. UNLIKE ARTISTS WHO SAW ADULTS AS THEIR AUDIENCE, KEITH BELIEVED THAT FINE ART SHOULD BE FOR YOUNG PEOPLE AND SPENT COUNTLESS HOURS DRAWING AND PAINTING FOR AND WITH THEM.

CHILDREN

COLLEEN ERNST WAS STRUGGLING.

The art teacher at Horn Elementary School in Iowa City was trying to teach her class how to draw the human figure, but it wasn't going so well. The students became tense and anxious as soon as they put pen to paper.

She understood the problem. "The students have this standard even by the third grade that the human figure has to be realistic," she explained. "By the time they're in sixth grade, they're real uptight about it. It's hard to convince them that their [nonrealistic] drawings are OK."

What to do?

Colleen had an idea. She knew of a successful young artist whose human figures were far from realistic. Maybe he could come and help her class loosen up and draw freely.

So Colleen sat down and wrote him a note.

Dear Mr. Haring . . .

In March 1984, Keith held a drawing workshop at Horn Elementary. Laying down long sheets of white papers, he invited the students to grab a marker or crayon and stand on either side of the paper.

Then he gave instructions for something like musical chairs. At his signal, the students were to approach the paper and start drawing whatever they wanted, but when he said *Switch*, they were to move to another spot and add to a drawing that was already there.

Horn Elementary students watching Keith paint a mural during his second visit to the school, in 1989

On cue, the students attacked. One drew a hairy eyeball, another drew a flower with a face, and another drew a green-eyed monster. Keith joined in, sketching a creature that resembled a caterpillar.

Switch!

"Don't be upset when someone else turns your car into a dog," Keith added.

Moving on to Keith's caterpillar, student Jobin Chien found the freedom exhilarating. "You don't exactly have to think of things to draw—you just put the pencil on paper and start."

Colleen was amazed at the creative juices flowing from her students. "They don't seem to have any blocks today," she said. "This experience is going to have the effect of freeing them up. And it's helping me figure out a way to loosen them up in art class."

On occasion, Keith thought about becoming an art teacher.

"I would love to be a teacher because I love children and I think that not enough people respect children or understand how important they are," he wrote in his journal.

"Children are the bearers of life in its simplest and most joyous form,"

Keith explained. "Children are color-blind and still free of all the complications, greed, and hatred that will slowly be instilled in them through life."

Beyond that, he took pleasure in their silly humor, their wild imaginations, and their blunt honesty. Because they were so frank, children were his "hardest audience," he said.

Keith's love for young people had its roots in Kutztown.

At the age of twelve, he found himself sharing a bedroom with his newborn sister, Kristen. It was a peculiar arrangement that led to some of the most positive moments in his life.

When Kristen was a baby, Keith would gently lift her from her crib and hold her close. When she needed comforting, he would rock her back and forth. When bedtime approached, he would sing her lullabies.

"I was totally in love with this little girl!" he said.

As Kristen grew older, Keith would push her to the library in a stroller, telling her to read everything she could. Of course, the two would also draw and paint together, using the switch game for extra excitement.

Keith also thought about being a father.

"I don't think I'm going to have a wife, but I would like to have a baby sometime," he said in 1983. "I really like babies. I'm not sure when or how, but it would be great."

Although fatherhood proved elusive, Keith became a godfather to several children, including Zena, the daughter of Kenny and Tereza Scharf, and Colin, the son of Kermit and Lisa Oswald.

• • •

In May 1987, Keith made sure that his new goddaughter, Madison Arman, the daughter of his friends Yves and Debbie, would be surrounded by art. He painted her highchair and crib, and he decorated her nursery walls with colorful cows and monkeys and chickens. Keith dearly loved baby Madison. He said that she looked like "a little baby lamb that hasn't grown any fur yet."

Sister Kristen painting Keith, 1973.

Two years later, Yves died in a car crash in Spain, and Keith flew straightway to be with Madison and Debbie. It was a terribly painful experience for him, eased by the times he held his goddaughter.

"I sang Madison to sleep, which was one of the most beautiful moments I've had in a long time," he wrote in his journal. "The feeling of holding a baby and rocking and singing them to sleep is one of the most satisfying feelings I have ever felt. I'll never know the pleasure of having this experience with my own child, but the times I've done it with Zena [Scharf] and Madison or my little sister, Kristen, are deeply embedded in my memory."

In her adult years, Kristen watched her brother singing lullabies to their nieces. "He loved doing that," she recalled. "If there was a baby around, he loved to put it to sleep. He found that moment magical—the release that happens in a child, that softness."

"The reason that the 'baby' has become my logo or signature is that it is the purest and most positive experience of human existence," Keith said.

On May 4, 1989, Keith popped a video into the videocassette recorder in his studio.

As he and his friends gathered around the TV, an image of Colleen Ernst's art students at Horn Elementary School appeared on the screen. The happy group broke out in song: "Happy birthday to you! Happy birthday to you! Happy birthday, dear Keith! Happy birthday to you!"

"It was the best birthday present I got," Keith told the students when visiting them later that month. It had been five years since his first visit to Horn, and thanks to another invitation from Colleen, he was back to share a slide show about his art and to paint a mural in the reading corner of the school's media center.

The students sat on the floor and watched in amazement as Keith started the mural without any sketches to guide him. Using his typical bright colors, he painted a book with a face and a big thought bubble coming from it. Inside the bubble were all kinds of fun things—ducks, clowns, and cartoon characters.

The students smiled and giggled when Keith added a special message next to his signature: "A book full of fun for my friends at [a picture of a horn] School!!"

Keith had long known that he could evoke smiles and giggles from children.

"It's probably from having a funny face to begin with—and looking and acting like a kid," he mused. "And kids can relate to my drawings, because of the simple lines."

Keith's mural at Horn Elementary, 1989.

But Keith also pointed to something deeper—a special bond he sensed between him and children.

"*I love life*," he wrote in his journal. "I appreciate everything that has happened, especially the *gift of life* I was given that has created a silent bond between me and children. Children can sense this 'thing' in me. . . . *They know*."

In Keith's mind, this "thing" he shared with children—a joyful and loving fascination with everyday life—made him unique in the art world.

"It is this quality that separates me from other artists," he wrote. "Maybe you don't understand this now, but you will. I am different."

Two years after writing these words, Keith and five hundred art students from Chicago public high schools joined together to paint a mural on a 488-foot-long wall.

Near the end of the event, a student told Keith one of the best things he'd ever heard—"I can tell by watching you paint that you really love life."

In January 1990, eight-year-old Russell Renner checked out the mural that Keith had painted on the interior walls of Schneider Children's Hospital on Long Island, New York.

The mural included one fun character after another—a hopping bunny, a smiling crescent moon, a cheery dachshund, a girl holding a lollipop and sticking her tongue out. Also making a prominent appearance was the crawling baby with a thermometer in its mouth.

"He's eating the thing!" said Russell, on his way to a medical appointment.

Later, when leaving the hospital building, the little boy probably spotted Keith's brightly painted sculptures of three tumbling human figures. Or maybe they were kids doing gymnastics. Or breakers dancing to the beat.

The hospital's chief of staff, Philip Lanzkowsky, found Keith's work a wonderful offering. "It puts [the children] at ease," he said. "It diverts them from the trauma of being in an institution."

Keith expanded on the point. "I think there's a lot of things about art that have a lot to do with healing," he said. "It's definitely helpful for children to be around art."

● ● ●

Keith completed this 10-story-high mural of Lady Liberty with the CityKids Foundation in 1986.

Looking back at the times he made art with children, the murals he painted in schools and hospitals across the globe, and his strong connections with young people—Keith felt certain about one thing:

"Whatever else I am, I'm sure I, at least, have been a good companion to a lot of children and maybe have touched their lives in a way that will be passed on through time, and taught them a kind of simple lesson of sharing and caring. . . . Somehow I think this is the reason I'm still alive."

In 1987, when he wrote these words, the topic of life and death was front and center in Keith's mind.

Two of his best friends had died at the beginning of the year—Andy Warhol and Pop Shop manager Bobby Breslau. Bobby had died of AIDS, a horrific disease that was snatching the lives of hundreds of artists in Lower Manhattan.

Just as troubling, other friends had recently confronted life-threatening drug addictions—including a young assistant whom Keith admired and loved.

reaction to a tag—"LA II"—that he saw in numerous places on the Lower East Side.

"It stood out because it was absolutely perfect and beautiful," he said.

Keith mentioned the tag to his friend, Futura, who knew about everyone in the graffiti world, and he spread word that Keith wanted to meet LA II.

Before long, a fourteen-year-old boy of Puerto Rican descent showed up at a site where Keith and other graffiti artists were painting a mural.

"Yo, why you lookin' for LA?" the boy asked Keith.

"You *know* LA II?"

"Yeah, it's me!"

Keith wasn't convinced. After all, LA II was so accomplished, and the boy standing in front of him was so young.

"Prove to me you're LA II," he said.

The boy took one of Keith's markers and wrote his signature.

Keith was shocked.

LA II was Angel Ortiz.

LA stood for "Little Angel." And the II? "I put the II, because the real LA is Los Angeles, California—and that's LA I," Angel explained. "So LA II—it's me."

Keith was so impressed with the quality of LA II's tag that he invited the teenager to collaborate with him on numerous occasions. From 1980 to 1985, the two artists worked together on murals, sculptures, pottery, and more, the pieces often showing Keith's bold lines surrounded by LA II's mesmerizing squiggles.

Keith and LA II always split their profits, each seeing the other as essential to the final products. They also saw each other as friends. When looking back on the remarkable collaboration, Ortiz said, "My relationship with Keith has always been about friendship first and the artistic aspect was and will always be secondary."

11 CRACK IS WACK

CRACK IS WACK, 1986.

KEITH WAS A REGULAR DRUG USER, BUT HE WAS VERY WARY OF A TOXIC AND HIGHLY ADDICTIVE FORM OF COCAINE CALLED CRACK. THE CRACK EPIDEMIC DESTROYED LIVES AND NEIGHBORHOODS IN NEW YORK AND OTHER CITIES IN THE 1980S, AND KEITH PAINTED SEVERAL MURALS TO RAISE AWARENESS AND ENCOURAGE PEOPLE TO STAY AWAY FROM THE DRUG.

DRUGS

IT WAS ANOTHER NIGHT OF SWEATY DANCING AT THE PARADISE
Garage in 1985, and Benny Soto was having the time of his life. As he checked
out his fellow dancers, the Puerto Rican teenager kept seeing a most peculiar
thing—an image of a crawling baby on T-shirts and buttons.

*What **is** that?* he wondered.

His friends told him about Keith and his art show at Tony Shafrazi's nearby
gallery, and Benny decided to stop by.

Wow!

He was immediately taken by the colorful art, the party atmosphere, and
the featured artist. In a one-on-one chat, he impressed Keith so much that
Keith snagged a nearby paper bag and wrote his phone number on it, adding a
small drawing of a dancing figure.

Call me.

Before long, Benny was Keith's studio assistant.

The job was great. Benny ran errands, delivered paintings, and stretched canvases.

"Keith could get a little bitchy if I didn't get the measurements right," he recalls with a laugh. But the snappishness was rare, and it never lasted long.

Benny loved working with Keith, partly because it introduced him to opportunities he had never envisioned.

"I was really poor," Benny says. "I was from the South Bronx, and a lot of people there felt trapped, like there was no way out. But Keith showed me

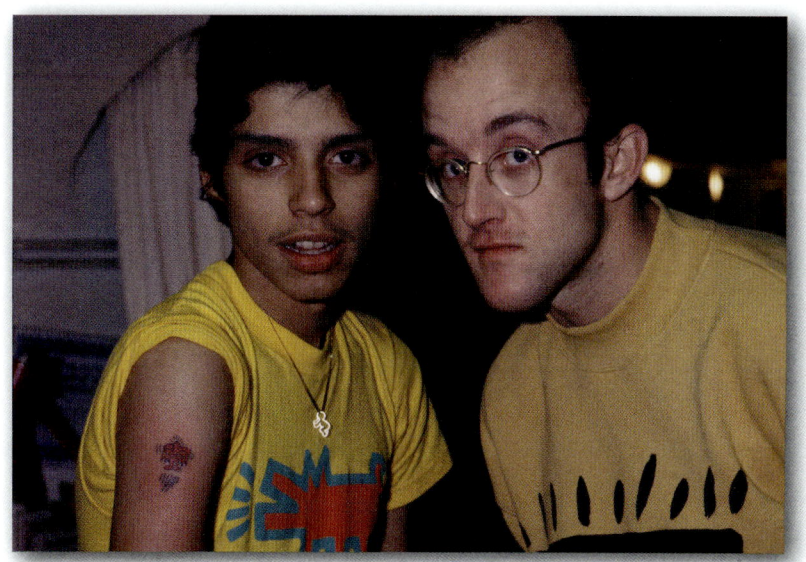

Keith gave Benny a tattoo in Amsterdam, Holland, 1986. It was the only tattoo he made.

that I didn't have to be a prisoner of my circumstances. He took my blinders off and gave me a whole new way to see the world. To see it as a place for creating something new. To see and appreciate art. To become open-minded. To appreciate differences in people."

Keith and Benny became close friends. The two traveled together, and Benny enjoyed access to Keith's inner circle, including Andy Warhol. One night, Keith, Benny, and Andy went to see *Pee-Wee's Big Adventure*, starring Keith's friend, comedian Paul Reubens.

Drugs were around, of course, and Benny partook.

Eventually, he tried crack cocaine, a highly addictive stimulant typically smoked in a pipe. Crack was so dangerous that even Keith—who tried it but usually snorted cocaine in its white powder form—was wary of it. "Crack makes you totally schizo-phrenic, aggressive, and irrationally obsessed with wanting more," he said.

That's what happened to Benny—he wanted more.

Keith knew about Benny's use of crack, and he noticed that his assistant was showing up late for work and that he wasn't as reliable as he had been.

So one day in 1986, Keith called Benny at home.

"I think you're an addict, and you need to get help," Keith said.

Benny was shaken. This was the first time anyone had dared to tell him that. Yes, he had missed work and lost friends and money, but he had never considered his drug use to be a life-threatening problem.

Holy shit! Benny said to himself. *Am I an addict?*

Keith remembered the moment as "really distressing because [Benny] was really brilliant and the best assistant that I had. Everyone at the office was totally fond of him and it was difficult for all of us."

Benny asked for help, and Keith and the studio staff rallied to his side. "We called these cocaine hotlines and got him to start seeing a counselor," Keith recalled.

Unfortunately, the therapy didn't work out, and Benny returned to his former habit. That was not uncommon among addicts, but Benny was disappointed with himself. "I felt like the worst piece of shit," he recalls. At his breaking point, he decided to enter a residential rehabilitation program.

Keith and others stepped up again. "We proceeded to take him from city agency to city agency, emergency room to emergency room, trying to get him admitted, because if you don't have insurance or a lot of money to go to an expensive clinic, then the only way you can get admitted to a program is through the emergency room of a hospital," Keith explained.

For various reasons, no hospital would admit him, but with Keith's assistance, Benny eventually received the help he needed. More important than Keith's financial help was Benny's own fierce resolve to defeat his demons and become a better person.

New York City, like many other urban areas, experienced a crack epidemic in the 1980s and 1990s. Crack houses, where the drug was manufactured, sold, and used, were prominent particularly in impoverished areas.

Making matters worse, at least as Keith saw it, President Reagan and his administration addressed the epidemic mostly by asking everyone to "just say no" to drugs, rather than by offering the financial resources required for moving people with addictions into drug-treatment programs.

Keith wanted to do something.

"Inspired by Benny, and appalled by what was happening in the country, but especially in New York, and seeing the slow reaction (as usual) of the government to respond, I decided I had to do an anti-crack painting."

On the morning of June 27, 1986, Keith, Benny, and Juan Rivera filled a rented van with ladders and paint cans and brushes. Juan drove the van to East Harlem Park, where the wall of a handball court stood right next to FDR Drive, a road used by more than 100,000 vehicles every day.

Keith had chosen this wall because it was easily visible to people driving into Manhattan from places north, including the Bronx, which was infamous for crack. Plus, there were lots of crack houses in neighborhoods near the park.

Jumping out of the van, the three men surveyed their cement canvas, propped up their ladders, and painted the wall florescent orange.

Keith then outlined the wall in black and painted "CRACK IS WACK" in the middle. To the right of the giant letters, he added a human figure hanging upside down, its feet bound by a rope and its head and arms dangling just inside the fierce jaw of an alligator figure.

Not only was crack wack—it was also deadly.

The painting attracted a lot of attention even before it was finished.

"During the day, a lot of people from the neighborhood came to watch," Keith said. "Cars went past, honking their horns and cheering because of the message." Several police officers also stopped by to check out the work.

At the end of the day, after the van was packed, Keith, Juan, and Benny were pleased with their work. It was just what they had hoped for.

"The thing that was needed most at that time was really public awareness, to prevent other people from getting involved with [crack]," Keith explained.

But then trouble arrived. A police car pulled up, and an officer asked Keith whether he had the city's permission to paint the wall.

Nooo.

The officer arrested him, charging him with defacing public property.

On September 18, Keith appeared in court, facing the possibility of up to three months in prison and a $500 fine.

By this point, the wall had attracted national attention. "Every time the news did a story on crack, they would flash to the board as a visual," Keith recalled. "NBC did a public service announcement using it as a background."

News outlets had even asked Keith for his thoughts about President Reagan's war on drugs. "The sentiment is right, but it's misdirected," Keith said. "Supposedly, Reagan is patriotic and really cares. But if he really cared, he would have done something about drug rehab centers, instead of taking all the money out of communities that were facing drug problems."

Now standing before Judge Patricia Anne Williams, Keith pleaded guilty to a reduced charge of disorderly conduct. Sympathetic but stern, the judge told Keith that, despite his good intentions, he had clearly broken the law—and the law was the law. She then ordered him to pay a fine of twenty-five dollars.

No jailtime!

"I was relieved, I guess," Keith said.

A week later, he was furious. Someone had vandalized the mural, changing the "Crack Is Wack" message to "Crack Is It." Keith suspected that the perpetrators were "probably crack users themselves."

The New York City Parks Department learned about the defaced mural before Keith did, and park employees covered the entire mural with gray paint, upsetting not only Keith, but also Park Commissioner Henry J. Stern.

The commissioner was a fan of the original mural, and he invited Keith to repaint it, this time with full support from the city, including a van, ladders, paint—and the assurance of no arrests.

Keith accepted, and in early October 1986, he painted a mural with the same message—"Crack Is Wack"—but with different detail. Below the bold message, he painted fire, distressed and dying human figures, and a skeleton holding a crack pipe that resembled a ticking time bomb. It was one of the scariest paintings in Keith's entire body of work.

While crack continued to rage across New York City, another deadly drug was wrecking thousands of lives—including Jean-Michel Basquiat's.

On August 12, 1988, Jean-Michel was stretched out on the floor next to his bed.

His skin was hot and he was unconscious.

Kelle Inman, Jean-Michel's girlfriend at the time, and their mutual friend, Kevin Bray, rushed to his side. "We picked him up and turned him over," Kevin said. "We shook him, and we just kept trying to revive him."

Then the ambulance crew arrived. They gave Jean-Michel an IV, or intravenous therapy, and used their defibrillators, trying to shock him back to life.

Nothing worked.

The crew then transported him to the emergency room at Cabrini Medical Center on East Nineteenth Street.

The hospital staff could do nothing.

Jean-Michel was pronounced dead on arrival.

Keith was visiting his parents in Kutztown when Jean-Michel's father, Gerard, telephoned with the news. Heartbroken and stunned, Keith called his childhood friend, Kermit Oswald, and a few others to mark Jean-Michel's life with a bonfire.

The next morning, Keith and Kermit witnessed a triangle of white butterflies fluttering above the white ashes of the fire. "That's Jean-Michel!" Keith said, revealing his mystical side.

Back in New York, Keith channeled his grief into painting. The result, *A Pile of Crowns for Jean-Michel Basquiat*, depicted a pile of three-pointed crowns, Jean-Michel's tag, surrounded by a red-and-black triangle sitting atop what appeared to be ashes. When Kermit saw the painting, he was sure the rising crowns looked just like the butterflies from the bonfire.

About a month before Jean-Michel died, he and Keith had run into each other on Broadway in Lower Manhattan.

Keith was snapping photographs for *Spin* magazine, and he asked Jean-Michel if he could take his picture. Jean-Michel agreed, but rather than standing there and smiling, he lay down on a subway grate and closed his eyes. Keith clicked away, noticing how peaceful his friend looked.

Before taking off, Jean-Michel said that he was kicking heroin and planning his next projects. Then, he asked Keith whether the troubling rumor was true.

"It's only as true as I look right now," Keith replied.

What was true?

Keith was HIV positive.

A Gift from Keith

"After I got clean, I went back to see Keith," Benny says. He wasn't exactly sure how the visit would go. "After all, I had messed up so badly."

But the reunion turned out beautifully. Keith was delighted to see his old friend, and his face lit up with the biggest smile.

For Christmas that year, Keith surprised Benny with a pair of Nike sneakers. Keith was a sneakerhead extraordinaire, so Benny knew this was a gift from the heart.

To top it off, Keith had written a special message on the box: "I love you and I'm looking forward to the new revised Benny Soto. Here's to a fresh start in 89!"

"I was blown away," Benny says. "I wanted him to see me that way. I wanted him to love me. I wanted . . . to be forgiven. He gave me all that, and more."

Today, Benny is a successful businessman.

12 STOP AIDS

STOP AIDS, 1989.

Keith created the stop AIDS poster after he was diagnosed as HIV-positive. Keith publicly came out as a person with AIDS, made art to raise public awareness, and joined a protest organization called ACT UP New York.

HIV

IT WAS THREE IN THE MORNING, TOKYO TIME, AND KEITH WAS still up, reading *Cities on a Hill*, a popular book by Frances FitzGerald.

Her portrayal of the Castro neighborhood in San Francisco in the 1980s was fascinating, but it was also troubling, especially the part about the gay man who searched his body for the purple splotches caused by a rare skin cancer called Kaposi's sarcoma.

For people with HIV—the virus that causes AIDS—the dreaded spots were signs that they might develop full-blown AIDS.

The first news reports of AIDS had appeared in 1981.

For the next two years, no one knew for certain that AIDS was caused by a virus, but it was crystal clear that its symptoms—Kaposi's sarcoma, pneumonia, lymphoma, and more—were deadly.

Although it was not a gay disease, AIDS hit the gay community especially hard, including the Lower East Side, where Keith saw many of his friends and acquaintances contracting the devastating virus.

Keith was diagnosed as HIV positive in 1987, and he had long thought he would find a splotch.

During his time in New York, he had been involved with many different men. "I was major into experimenting," he recalled. "If I didn't get [AIDS], no one would."

Ominously, by the time Keith was reading *Cities on a Hill*, his ex-partner, Juan DuBose, had been diagnosed with full-blown AIDS.

No one wanted to pick and scrape at death, but reading about the man in the book, Keith searched his body.

There it was, on his leg, a tiny purple splotch.

"I immediately got paranoid," he said.

Back in New York, Keith called his doctor.

Just before the appointment, he found another splotch, this one on his arm. Fear became unavoidable. Perhaps the splotches would soon be everywhere, even on his face. Maybe he would be confined to bed. Maybe he would die.

Keith's doctor checked out the lesions, took tissue samples, and sent them off for a biopsy, a special examination for cancer cells, with results expected in a week or so.

Rather than sitting on his hands, Keith headed to another doctor for a blood test that would show his T4-cell count. T4 cells keep the body immune from infections, and studies showed that a low count was symptomatic of HIV erupting into AIDS.

Sure enough, Keith's count was low. If there was any time to wring his hands, it was now.

Within the week, the biopsy results were in—yes, it was Kaposi's sarcoma.

Keith's doctor wrote a prescription for a potent drug called AZT. In a best-case scenario, the drug would slow the progression of AIDS.

"I went over to the East River and sat and cried and cried and cried," Keith said later.

Keith with what is probably a Kaposi's sarcoma lesion on his right arm, New York City, 1989.

He had every reason to break down. At that time, people with AIDS were expected to die. No doubt about it—it was just a matter of time.

Only when he could cry no more did Keith look ahead.

As he put it, "You realize that this is not the end right there, and that there are other things, and you've got to continue, and you've got to figure out how you're going to deal with it, confront it, and face it."

Back home, he shared the news with Juan Rivera.

It was already a difficult time for the couple—their relationship was on the rocks.

Keith said that although the two had a lot of fun together, they didn't have much in common, while Juan said that the problem was Keith's constant need to be on the move, and to be adored by lots of men.

"Because of the crisis in my life, I start to need more intellectual companionship," Keith later explained. "So the more I'm struggling with the situation that starts to unfold, the more I need to talk to someone with whom I can have an intellectual relationship."

That "someone" had already appeared in Keith's life.

Three months earlier, with an invitation arranged by Keith's assistant, Gil Vazquez—an aspiring seventeen-year-old DJ from Spanish Harlem—stepped into Keith's studio.

Gil knew of Keith's subway drawings. "I knew the baby," he recalls. "I knew the dog. I knew the Pop Shop. But I didn't know about his activism or who he was as a person."

The studio was colorful and busy. Artworks filled the walls, staffers darted here and there, and T-shirts waited to be given away. Keith was hammering nails into a reproduction of the *Mona Lisa*.

"And I am just in awe, in complete awe," Gil recalls. "And [Keith] was super nice. I had all these questions. And I just started to learn about the man. We somehow became very fast friends."

For his part, Keith found Gil "incredibly beautiful," as well as "smart, sympathetic, and clever."

And straight—as in, "not gay."

The two began "a friendship *not* based on sex," Keith said. But it *was* based on love. Both developed deep love for each other as they traveled the world, visiting art museums, dancing at nightclubs, and talking about everything under the sun. When Keith shared news about his diagnosis, Gil turned out to be "incredibly compassionate."

Not everyone understood the sexless relationship, but Keith was unfazed.

"All I know is [Gil] makes me happier and smarter than anyone I ever met in my life," Keith wrote in his journal.

On February 2, 1989, Keith visited Juan DuBose—his first longtime partner—as he lay dying in a hospital. AIDS had wrecked his body.

The former couple talked for a long time. "When I leave, Juan reaches up to kiss me goodbye," Keith recalled. "At the door, I turn and wave goodbye to him. The next morning, Juan's mother calls to say Juan has died."

At the funeral, Keith was initially afraid to look at Juan's body in the open casket, but when he dared, he was taken aback by how beautiful and peaceful Juan looked.

Another reaction also came to the surface, according to Keith's friend Bruno Schmidt. "I remember Keith staring at the coffin and saying, 'Well, soon it will be me there.'"

About three weeks later, Keith stood in front of a slanted cement wall in El Raval, an impoverished neighborhood in Barcelona, Spain, that was notorious for drug use and prostitution.

After cranking the volume on his boombox, Keith started painting a red giant snake twisting around a hypodermic syringe and chasing human figures, including one with a baby. Another painted figure appeared dead, and another was putting a condom on the snake's tail. Two figures in the shape of scissors were attempting to cut the snake in half.

Lots of local kids gathered around, peppering Keith with questions and asking for more of the crawling baby buttons he was handing out. One of the boys appointed himself as Keith's protector and shielded the artist so he could work without interruption. The media turned out, too.

About five hours later, as he neared the end of the long mural, Keith painted human figures dancing and holding hands under the words "*Todos Juntos Podemos Parar el SIDA*" ("Together We Can Stop AIDS").

While journaling that night, Keith described the mural as "an attempt to reach out to the people who actually live there." People who used intravenous drugs. Or had unsafe sex. Or did both. "The message was one of education so that people will be more careful and conscious of AIDS and hopefully avoid it."

Keith and kids at his first AIDS mural in Barcelona, Spain, 1989.

• • •

The work in El Raval was the first mural Keith made that directly addressed AIDS, but since 1982, when he had made art for an AIDS fundraiser at the Paradise

Garage, he had been using his art to raise awareness about the disease. By at least 1985, he was also publicly advocating for safe sex.

Keith disagreed sharply with those who tried to fight AIDS merely by urging people to abstain from sex. "I think it's unrealistic to tell people not to have sex, because it's not going to happen," he said.

Those words reflected his own experience. After news reports that AIDS was contracted from sexual activity, in May 1981, long before Keith was diagnosed as HIV positive, he did not stop having sex. Nor did he stop having sex with numerous partners. Instead, he sought to reduce the exchange of bodily fluids, by engaging in safe-sex practices.

He tried to persuade others to do the same, mostly by designing safe-sex posters that various organizations then distributed to the public. One showed two males masturbating each other—an image that could be displayed only in select places. Other posters featured "Debbie Dick," a smiley character who said, "Wear Rubbers!"

Keith also attended meetings of the AIDS Coalition to Unleash Power (ACT UP)—a militant group known for being loud and in your face—at the Lesbian and Gay Community Services Center in the West Village.

In March 1989, after learning about an upcoming protest at City Hall, he approached Peter Staley, head of ACT UP's fundraising.

"Peter, I really want to help with this action, financially," Keith said. "Can you stop by my studio? I kind of have a cash business these days."

"Sure!" Peter said.

When Peter showed up, he was impressed. "The studio was this big beehive of a space," he recalls. "And there was Keith, covered in paint, looking cute, and in charge of all his underlings."

After a quick greeting, Keith headed to a knapsack stashed in the corner, pulled out a huge wad of cash, and gave it to Peter. It was $10,000.

"And I very carefully put it in my bike bag and walked it as quickly as I could to our local bank branch," Peter says with a chuckle.

It was just one of the times when Keith helped fund ACT UP's campaigns against AIDS. He also wrote a fundraising letter that raised $70,000, donated artworks to the group, and gave them twenty thousand free copies of his famous "Ignorance = Fear / Silence = Death" poster.

● ● ●

On March 28, 1989, about three thousand protesters descended on City Hall Park in Manhattan to denounce Mayor Ed Koch's response to the AIDS crisis.

"Act up! Fight back! Fight AIDS!" the marchers yelled.

Keith carried a sign initially designed by artist Richard Deagle. Divided in four, the sign showed a picture of Koch, with pursed lips, in each quadrant. To the right of each photo was a viciously sarcastic message in red and black:

Keith at an ACT UP protest at City Hall, New York City, 1989.

"10,000 New York City AIDS Deaths—How'm I Doin'?" Koch often bragged about his success by brashly asking voters, "How'm I doin'?"

This was not Keith's first ACT UP protest. Two months earlier, he had joined a kiss-in demonstration in front of New York's St. Vincent's Hospital, because of a report that a homophobic staffer had mistreated a person with AIDS. Ron

Goldberg, ACT UP's chant leader, had made a beeline for Keith, thrilled at his one and only chance to kiss the famous artist.

● ● ●

In August 1989, Keith came out to the world as a person with AIDS.

Up to this point, he had joined public fights against the disease, but now, in an interview with David Sheff of *Rolling Stone* magazine, he revealed that he, too, had AIDS.

Why come out to the public?

Keith was disturbed by famous people who had hidden their diagnoses—the entertainer Liberace and actor Rock Hudson, for instance. Their silence had allowed the media to perpetuate the myth that AIDS was punishment for gay sex, Keith said.

So, by being open about his illness, Keith believed that he would be able to control his story and prevent the media from depicting it as morally shameful.

The interview was intense, with Keith sharing his raw feelings about how AIDS affected his life.

I have so many friends, kids that are friends. My godchildren. I have a lot of kids almost like my own. . . . I just can't imagine. I really, really, really don't want them to see me get the way that I've seen other people get. I don't know which is more noble: to fight to the end, until your last breath, no matter what you turn into, or to cut it off and die with dignity. I don't know which would leave a better impression in their minds. Would it be worse for them to know that you took your own life? Or to know, even if it wasn't pretty at the end, that you fought and had a will to fight and tried to survive?

Four months after the interview, on December 10, 1989, Keith fought on by participating in an ACT UP protest targeting Cardinal John O'Connor, the Catholic archbishop of New York, for his vocal opposition to using condoms to prevent the transmission of HIV.

The protest had two main strategies—to confront O'Connor during Sunday mass inside St. Patrick's Cathedral, and to stage a larger protest outside the cathedral. Keith stayed outside, along with 4,500 other protesters, many of them gravely ill and yet braving the freezing weather to highlight the importance of condoms as tools for fighting AIDS.

Kenny Scharf wished his friend would take better care of himself—that he would stop burning the candle at both ends. Although Keith did not accept the advice, he did tend to his personal health in his own ways.

While continuing to take AZT, he also tried experimental drugs, even injecting himself with a drug called interferon.

It didn't work.

Staring at death, Keith continued to paint whenever he could. He had read a book about self-healing and believed that painting could help conquer his disease. "I really want to . . . try to heal myself by painting," he wrote in his journal. "I think I could actually do it."

"The hardest thing is just knowing that there's so much more stuff to do," he said. "I'm so scared that one day I'll wake up and I won't be able to do it."

Despite his efforts, healing proved elusive.

Large Kaposi's sarcoma lesions covered parts of his body, including the inside of his mouth, and he developed lymphoma, a cancer that signaled the advance of AIDS. Too tired to work, he began staying home.

But one day in early February 1990, Keith mustered all his strength and returned to his studio. Julia Gruen, his assistant and studio manager, watched him struggle to draw. Painting was out of the question. "He was just too weak," she said.

More shocking was Keith's voice. "When he tried to speak, he was sort of scratching and screeching, with no sound coming out. It was heartbreaking."

By now, Keith was even too weak to receive additional medical treatment. His body was wasting away, and his eyes seemed bigger than ever.

Word spread that the end was near. Family and friends showed up at his apartment, showering him with love and attention. Gil Vazquez stayed by Keith's bedside; so did their mutual friend, Lysa Cooper.

"There were now periods when Keith would be in a delirium," Julia Gruen recalled. "He just didn't know who anybody was. He didn't know who his mother was. It was unbearable."

On February 15, Keith tried to draw his crawling baby.

He could barely hold the black marker.

"He was really struggling, toiling to have control of the line," Gil said.

Some of Keith's last drawings of the crawling baby, 1990.

Lysa Cooper and Kenny Scharf kept feeding him one blank piece of paper after another.

"You could see in his face how frustrating it was for him," Gil said. "Finally, he drew this baby that was not really completed."

That night, the home nurse noticed that Keith's liver and kidney functions were failing—a sure and certain sign that death was close.

She woke up Keith's parents, Joan and Allen, in the downstairs bedroom. They rushed to their son's side, crawled into bed with him, and held him close.

Before the sun could rise, Keith drew his last breath.

He was only thirty-one years old.

EPILOGUE

REBELLIOUS

ON MAY 4, 1990, THIRTY-TWO YEARS AFTER HIS BIRTH, ABOUT A thousand people gathered for Keith's memorial service at the Cathedral of St. John the Divine in Manhattan. The gathering offered family and friends a chance to reflect on Keith's life and legacy.

In his brief comments, art curator Jeffrey Deitch said that Keith's work "screamed with dire warnings, but his message was optimistic."

Guests nodded their heads in easy agreement.

Keith's work did indeed warn of so many things—nuclear weapons, racial injustice, police brutality, anti-queer politicians, and so much more.

At the same time, it rebelled against the notion that we are helpless and cannot break the chains that oppress us. In one drawing after another, Keith told us . . .

"RESIST!"

● ● ●

A Keith-inspired poster at an LGBTQ march protesting then-President Donald Trump's immigration policies in New York City, 2017.

Keith's sister Kay spoke at the service, sharing a personal reflection on the joy and passion that her brother brought to life.

> I learned a lot from my big brother: That a wall was meant to be drawn on, a Saturday night was meant for partying, and that life is meant for celebrating! Keith showed me that it is possible to live what you believe.

Keith's battle with AIDS taught me that every day is worth living. When he tested HIV positive, instead of complaining about the burden of the disease and in answer to a comment on how hard it must be to live with that knowledge, he replied, "No, it just makes everything that happens now so much better, because you never know when you're doing something for the last time. So you live each day as if it were the last."

Kay's heartfelt message resonated deeply with all those who loved her brother—especially the young people.

Keith was right about them. They could sense his love of life. They could see it in his paintings—the fun swirls, the comical characters, the simple line. They could detect it in his face—his raised eyebrows, his big eyes, his goofy smile. And they could feel it when he sat down with them and said . . .

Let's draw!

Keith's longtime friends, Kenny Scharf and Ann Magnuson, lightened the memorial service's mood even more by doing an Academy Awards skit in the zany spirit of Club 57.

After nominating Keith for various awards, including "best go-go dancer," the two friends delivered their final punchline: "And the winner is . . . everyone who knew Keith Haring."

The audience beamed.

Let's dance!

Seven years later, in June 1997, the Whitney Museum of American Art in New York City held a retrospective on Keith's art—a look back at the pieces he had created over his lifetime. The show featured more than two hundred works, including drawings, paintings, murals, and sculptures.

"There may never be another Haring retrospective on this scale; his work isn't meant for museum scrutiny," wrote *New York Times* critic Holland Cotter.

Since his death, Keith's artwork has had one-person shows in museums across the globe, from Sweden to Brazil to Japan, and today his drawings and paintings hang in prestigious museums everywhere.

But some museums have chosen not to honor his work.

The Museum of Modern Art (MoMA), arguably the most important modern art museum in the world, continues to neglect Keith's work. MoMA's holdings include several pieces by Keith, but they rarely go on public view—even though the MoMA Design Store has more than forty separate Keith Haring items for sale, including the inflatable baby.

Would Keith care?

It might be satisfying to say no, but remember that in 1988 he complained in his journal that MoMA had not shown even one of his works.

Keith cared very much about how museums treated his work—he wanted the respect that he and so many others, including Andy Warhol, thought he deserved.

Nevertheless, because Keith was a rebellious populist at heart, perhaps he would be thrilled beyond words to see that his legacy is alive and well "on the street"—in his numerous murals and sculptures, of course, but also on T-shirts and sweatshirts, baseball caps and backpacks, and skateboards and sneakers—even tattoos.

Wherever it is, in elite museums or everyday streets, Keith's art constantly reminds us of his belief that art is for everybody and that its role is to uplift us and agitate for peace and justice.

Perhaps that hints at our role, too. Perhaps our role in this moment is to take Keith's art more seriously than ever. To uplift one another. To fight for peace and justice.

And, at last, to create a world where every baby, no matter where they are born, is swaddled and rocked and loved as if there is no tomorrow.

Extra Paint and Brushes

Because this biography is rather short, here are extra sources to help you finish painting your own picture of Keith's life and art.

The best social media site:

haringkids.com

Five excellent books written mostly for adults:

Jeffrey Deitch, Suzanne Geiss, and Julia Gruen, *Keith Haring*

Brad Gooch, *Radiant: The Life and Line of Keith Haring*

John Gruen, *Keith Haring: The Authorized Biography*

Keith Haring, *Keith Haring Journals*

Ricardo Montez, *Keith Haring's Line: Race and the Performance of Desire*

Three wonderful documentaries:

Drawing the Line: A Portrait of Keith Haring, directed by Elizabeth Aubert Schlumberger

Keith Haring: Street Art Boy, directed by Ben Anthony

The Universe of Keith Haring, directed by Christina Clausen

And one super-fun picture book by Keith's sister:

Kay A. Haring, *Keith Haring: The Boy Who Just Kept Drawing*

TiMELiNE

1958
Born in Reading, Pennsylvania.

Begins to scribble.

1962
Draws cartoons.

1967
Dreams of becoming an artist in France.

1970
Creates *Peterson & Co. & Friends,* a political cartoon strip.

Builds first art studio with Kermit Oswald.

1972
Joins the Christian born-again movement.

Plasters Kutztown with religious stickers.

1973
Starts taking illegal drugs.

Makes abstract art.

1976
Falls in love with Susan Kriske.

Graduates from Kutztown Area High School.

Attends the Ivy School of Professional Art in Pittsburgh.

1977
Drops out of Ivy.

Hitchhikes to San Francisco with Susan.

Moves back to Pittsburgh with Susan.

Has first professional art show at Fisher Scientific, a chemical company in Pittsburgh.[*]

Influenced by artists Jean Dubuffet and Pierre Alechinsky.

---

[*] For a helpful list of Keith's one-person and group exhibitions, as well as his special projects, see Jeffrey Deitch, Suzanne Geiss, and Julia Gruen, in cooperation with the Estate of Keith Haring, *Keith Haring* (New York: Rizzoli, 2014), 508–514. This book also includes numerous photographs and images of some of Keith's most important art.

1978

Comes out as gay.

Influenced by artist Christo's lecture.

Has show at the Pittsburgh Arts and Crafts Center.

Breaks up with Susan.

Leaves Pittsburgh.

Moves to the West Village in New York City.

Influenced by graffiti.

Attends the School of Visual Arts.

Sketches *Manhattan Penis Drawings for Ken Hicks*.

Moves to the East Village.

1979

Influenced by cut-up works of William Burroughs and Brion Gysin.

Reads poetry at Club 57.

Wheat-pastes 200 posters of excerpts from *Sex Guide to Married Life*.

Influenced by Jean-Michel Basquiat and SAMO©.

Creates numerous video projects.

1980

Curates art shows at Club 57.

Shows gay-themed works at *The Times Square Show*.

Creates visual language with new cartoonish images.

Shows new images at Club 57.

Draws crawling babies and dogs on the Lower East Side.

Wheat-pastes anti-Reagan and anti-Pope John Paul II posters.

Drops out of the School of Visual Arts.

Shows work at P.S. 122 studio.

Receives first significant notice from the New York press.

Draws on Johnnie Walker Red Label Scotch poster.

Starts chalk drawings in subway.

1981

Continues subway drawings.

Paints his first vase.

Receives attention in downtown and art publications.

Has first solo show at Westbeth Painters' Space.

Exhibits works at *New York/New Wave* show in Long Island City.

Receives positive acclaim in *Interview* magazine.

Curates art shows at the Mudd Club, including *Beyond Words*, a survey of the city's graffiti art.

Has a one-person show at Club 57.

Starts to sell his art to wealthy collectors, particularly Donald and Mera Rubell.

Visits Paradise Garage for the first time.

Falls in love with Juan DuBose.

Begins collaboration with Angel Ortiz (LA II).

Paints the three-eyed cartoon character for the first time.

Exhibits in group shows at the Tony Shafrazi Gallery and the Annina Nosei Gallery, both in Lower Manhattan.

Praised in "The Radiant Child," a major article in *Artforum*.

1982

Continues subway drawings.

Shows cartoon images on a lightboard in Times Square.

Provides art for AIDS fundraiser for the first time.

Starts to practice safer sex.

Hires gallerist Tony Shafrazi to represent his work.

Has first show in Europe (Rotterdam, Holland).

Exhibits at influential *Documenta 7* show in Kassel, Germany.

Draws and paints breakdancers.

Produces anti-nuclear poster for NYC protest.

Paints famous mural at East Houston Street and Bowery.

Appears on cover of *ARTNews*.

Paints on tarps.

Has first major solo show at the Tony Shafrazi Gallery.

1983

Continues subway drawings.

Has hip-hop-themed show at the Fun Gallery.

Meets Andy Warhol.

Trades artwork with Warhol for the first time.

Has show at Watari Gallery in Tokyo.

Shows for the first time at the Whitney Biennial in NYC.

Michael Stewart dies.

Paints the body of dancer Bill T. Jones.

Draws during Jones's dance performance in *Long Distance*.

Has show at prestigious Robert Fraser Gallery in London.

Has second solo show at the Tony Shafrazi Gallery.

1984

Continues subway drawings.

Publishes *Art in Transit* with Tseng Kwong Chi.

Accused of appropriating Aboriginal art while painting mural in Australia.

Madonna performs "Like a Virgin" at Keith's "Party of Life."

Paints the body of Grace Jones.

Creates cartoon pig for NYC's "Don't Be a Litter Pig" campaign.

Draws anti-Reagan art.

Paints Avenue D Candy Store.

1985

Ends subway drawing project.

Creates "Free South Africa" poster.

Paints "safe-sex" messages.

Makes art for Area and Palladium nightclubs.

Paints at Live Aid benefit concert to fight famine in Africa.

Shows political works at third solo show at the Tony Shafrazi Gallery.

Exhibits sculptures at the prestigious Leo Castelli Gallery in SoHo.

Assaulted by three men trying to tar and feather him.

Paints *Michael Stewart (USA for Africa)*.

Creates *The Ten Commandments*.

Has first one-person retrospective in Bordeaux, France.

1986

Falls in love with Juan Rivera.

Opens the Pop Shop.

Paints *Crack Is Wack* mural.

Creates Statue of Liberty banner with CityKids Foundation.

Paints the Berlin Wall.

1987

Has fourth one-person show at the Tony Shafrazi Gallery.

Pop Shop manager Bobby Breslau dies of AIDS.

Andy Warhol dies of cardiac arrythmia.

Completes multiple projects in Europe, including a piece for the Luna Luna amusement park.

Paradise Garage closes.

Paints mural at Schneider Children's Hospital.

Designs "AIDS IS POLITICAL-BIO-LOGICAL (GERM) WARFARE" T-shirt.

Paints mural at Carmine Street Pool.

Creates demon sperm in work with William Burroughs.

1988

Opens Pop Shop Tokyo.

Paints at Easter Egg Roll at the White House.

Creates children's mural at Grady Hospital in Atlanta, Georgia.

Paints mural with safe-sex and anti-drug messages in the Lower East Side.

Creates *Nina's Book of Little Things* for seven-year-old Nina Clemente.

Visits the Peace Museum in Hiroshima.

Diagnosed with AIDS-related symptoms.

Jean-Michel Basquiat dies.

Paints *Pile of Crowns for Jean-Michel Basquiat*.

Paints *Silence = Death* to spread AIDS message.

Has fifth solo art show at the Tony Shafrazi Gallery.

1989

Falls in love with Gil Vazquez.

Juan DuBose dies of AIDS.

Paints first AIDS mural in Barcelona.

Creates mural with 300 young people in Grant Park, Chicago, Illinois.

Paints *Once Upon a Time* at the Lesbian and Gay Community Services Center in the West Village.

Creates religious mural in Pisa, Italy.

Participates in ACT UP protests.

Comes out in ACT UP fundraising letter and *Rolling Stone* interview.

Paints *The Last Rainforest*.

1990

Dies of AIDS.

ACKNOWLEDGMENTS

Thanks to the Keith Haring Foundation for granting me permission to access and publish Keith's art and images. Special thanks to Anna Gurton-Wachter, the foundation's top-notch archivist, for being so helpful and patient.

Keith's three sisters—Kay Haring, Karen DeLong, and Kristen Haring—provided me with memories, family photos, and images of Keith's early artwork. I'm grateful for their generosity and kindness, and for their caring and thoughtful approach to their brother's legacy.

Danke to three volunteers at the Kutztown Area Historical Society—Karen DeLong, Craig Koller, and Brendan Strasser—for organizing a wonderful exhibit of Keith's life and art, introducing me to Keith's hometown friends, and teaching me about Keith's childhood and young adult years. This trio represents everything good about Kutztown history, and I highly recommend a trip to the society's museum.

Norton Young Readers is my dream publisher, and my gratitude extends to the A-team behind this book: Hana Anouk Nakamura, art director and designer; Kristin Allard, associate editor; Naomi Duttweiler, marketing manager; Rebecca Munro, senior project editor; and Delaney Adams, production manager.

My editor, Simon Boughton, suggested that I rethink my initial approach. "Why not try something unconventional, like Keith's life?" he said. That was a very fine idea, and it helps explain why I'm grateful for the opportunity to work with Simon.

The idea of using twelve pictures as entry points into Keith's life came from my smart agent, John Rudolph, of Dystel, Goderich & Bourret. My appreciation for John's wise counsel is deep and wide.

The stunning artwork for this book includes photographs from esteemed artists, and I refer you to the credits for a list of all those who offered images. Special thanks to Muna Tseng, the accomplished dancer and choreographer, for providing me with images from the vast collection of her late brother, Tseng Kwong Chi.

Stories in this book come from numerous sources—interviews, conversations, documentaries, articles, books, and more. Thanks to all those who so generously spoke with me about Keith; you can find their names in the various chapters.

Two excellent books played an outsized role in helping me with stories: John Gruen's *Keith Haring: The Authorized Biography* and Brad Gooch's *Radiant: The Life and Line of Keith Haring*.

A shout-out to family members who provided their characteristic love and support—Karin, Jack, Elda, Jay, Nate, Bob, and George the Dog, all Longs—and to friends Sharon Herr, a proofreader extraordinaire, and Shea Tuttle, whose debut novel is on the way.

My deepest gratitude goes to Keith Haring for leaving a legacy that makes us smile and dance, inspires us to agitate for peace and justice, and insists that we honor and celebrate young people. He was exactly right when he wrote, "I am different."

Thanks, Keith, for being so different.

Notes

EPIGRAPHS

v   **"The freedom to be":** "Interview with Broad Street Studio," no date, KH 0794, Keith Haring Archives, Keith Haring Foundation, New York, New York.

v   **"I think the role":** *Drawing the Line: A Portrait of Keith Haring*, directed and produced by Elizabeth Aubert Schlumberger, 1989.

v   **"If you paint":** David Ramirez, "From Graffiti to Fame," *Arizona Republic*, December 15, 1986.

v   **"I'm still a kid at heart":** "Off the Wall with Keith and the Kids," video, WTTW, Chicago, 2018, accessed at https://www.pbs.org/video/off-the-wall-with-keith-and-the-kids-1tjcuz/.

PROLOGUE: ILLEGAL

2   **"You're under arrest":** CBS Sunday Morning, "From the Archives: Keith Haring," video, posted January 28, 2024, https://www.youtube.com/watch?v=8eE4Dm8EGTg.

1. RADIANT BABY: CHILDHOOD

6   **"I could never"** and **"He'd go through":** John Gruen, *Keith Haring: The Authorized Biography* (New York: Fireside, 1991), 4.

8   **"Instead of teaching":** *The Universe of Keith Haring*, directed by Christina Clausen, produced by Ian Ayres, Paolo Bruno, and Eric Elléna, 2008.

9   **"My father loved":** Gruen, *Keith Haring*, 9.

10 **"Perhaps in our"** and **"You could make":** Brad Gooch, *Radiant: The Life and Line of Keith Haring* (New York: Harper, 2024), 9.

11 **"good practice for":** *The Universe of Keith Haring*, Clausen, 2008.

12 **"He was always":** *Keith Haring: Street Art Boy*, directed by Ben Anthony, produced by Ben Anthony, Michael Kantor, Janet Lee, and Alice Rhodes, 2020.

12 **"Her whole idea":** Gooch, *Radiant*, 19.

12 **"I had glasses":** *Keith Haring*, Anthony, 2020.

12   **"He wasn't the":** Bruce Koller, in conversation with author, April 2, 2025.

13   **"insecure":** *Keith Haring*, Anthony, 2020.

14   **"sissy":** Martha Kuhns, in conversation with author, October 12, 2024.

14   **"When I grow"** and **"The reason is":** Jeffrey Deitch, Suzanne Geiss, and Julia Gruen, in cooperation with the Estate of Keith Haring, *Keith Haring* (New York: Rizzoli, 2014), 2–3.

15   **"I was really"** and **"I loved Walt":** *The Universe of Keith Haring*, Clausen, 2008. See also *Notes from the Pop Underground*, edited by Peter Belsito (Berkeley: The Gasp of San Francisco, 1985), 98.

16   **"It had a"** and **"It was a":** Gooch, *Radiant*, 27.

17   **"I'd say, 'Keith'":** Gruen, *Keith Haring*, 17.

17   **"[She] didn't make"** and **"But she was":** Gooch, *Radiant*, 35.

SIDEBAR: KEITH'S LINE

18   **"a simple way":** Matt Fussell, "The Elements of Art—'Line,'" *Virtual Instructor*, no date, accessed at https://thevirtualinstructor.com/line.html.

18   **"Keith Haring's line":** Jeffrey Deitch, email to author, March 11, 2025.

18   **"is a carved":** Gooch, *Radiant*, 259–260.

2. ROCK BANDS: TEENS

22   **"I distinctly remember":** John Gruen, *Keith Haring: The Authorized Biography* (New York: Fireside, 1991), 10.

23   **"Kolossal Kolor Pin-Up":** *16 Magazine*, February 1967, cover page.

23   **"I would cut":** Gruen, *Keith Haring*, 10.

25   **"I must have"** and **"I remember we":** Gruen, *Keith Haring*, 14.

27   **"I never really":** Gruen, *Keith Haring*, 10.

28   **"Turn that racket":** Quoted by Karen DeLong, in conversation with author, March 19, 2025.

29   **"I started doing"** and **"I started doing":** Brad Gooch, *Radiant: The Life and Line of Keith Haring* (New York: Harper, 2024), 40.

29   **"I was really"** and **"He loved pen":** Gruen, *Keith Haring*, 18.

31   **"I was a terror":** David Sheff, "Keith Haring: Just Say Know," *Rolling Stone*, August 10, 1989. Keith also said, "I was a shame to my parents." See Valerie Gladstone, "Keith Haring: Art's Bad Boy," *New York Daily News*, March 23, 1986.

31   **"terrorist rabbits":** Gruen, *Keith Haring*, 20.

31   **"very sweet, very":** Penny (Wagner) George, in conversation with author, May 7, 2025.

33   **"shit together":** Gruen, *Keith Haring*, 23.

34   **"I don't know":** Kristen Haring, in conversation with author, April 8, 2025.

34   **"Being under the influence":** *Notes from the Pop Underground*, edited by Peter Belsito (Berkeley: The Gasp of San Francisco, 1985), 98. See also Vince Aletti, "An Interview with Keith Haring," *Keith Haring: Future Primeval*, ed. Barry Blinderman (New York: Abbeville Press, 1990), 92.

SIDEBAR: MORE THAN A TERROR

35   **"*It was my eleventh*":** Karen DeLong, in conversation with author, March 19, 2025.

3. EMBRACING COUPLE: COMING OUT

38   **"But I always"** and **"I always knew":** John Gruen, *Keith Haring: The Authorized Biography* (New York: Fireside, 1991), 23.

40   **"The first thing":** *The Universe of Keith Haring*, directed by Christina Clausen, produced by Ian Ayres, Paolo Bruno, and Eric Elléna, 2008.

41   **"Your drawing should"** and **"You should not":** Robert Henri, *The Art Spirit* (Philadelphia: J.P. Lippincott, 1923; New York, Harper & Row, 1951), 242.

41   **"I would not":** "'Disco Designer' Haring Is Making His Way in Big Apple," Associated Press article, June 5, 1986.

42   **"The guy who"** and **"saw more faggots":** Keith Haring, *Keith Haring Journals* (New York: Viking, 1996), 3

43   **"Little by little":** Gruen, *Keith Haring*, 25.

44   **"I didn't even":** Daniel Drenger, "Art and Life: An Interview with Keith Haring," *Columbia Art Review* (Spring 1988): 52.

44   **"I knew *that*":** Gruen, *Keith Haring*, 31.

44   **"pseudo-Abstract Expressionist":** Keith Haring, interview by Terri Gross, *Fresh Air*, September 3, 1987, WHYY, Philadelphia.

47   **"It was sad"** and **"But it was":** Brad Gooch, *Radiant: The Life and Line of Keith Haring* (New York: Harper, 2024), 82.

47   **"I wasn't finding":** Ann Daly, "His Illegal Graffiti Wins Fame," *Pittsburgh Press*, October 18, 1983.

47   **"I wanted intensity":** Gruen, *Keith Haring*, 32.

4. CLONES GO HOME: NEW YORK CITY

50   **"It was like":** Jeffrey Deitch, Suzanne Geiss, and Julia Gruen, in cooperation with the Estate of Keith Haring, *Keith Haring* (New York: Rizzoli, 2014), 22.

53   **"Keith was having"** and **"He told me":** Brad Gooch, *Radiant: The Life and Line of Keith Haring* (New York: Harper, 2024), 92.

53   **"All those little":** John Gruen, *Keith Haring: The Authorized Biography* (New York: Fireside, 1991), 39.

53   **"a way to":** Deitch, Geiss, and Gruen, *Keith Haring*, 23.

56   **"First of all"** and **"I mean, everyone":** Gruen, *Keith Haring*, 43.

56   **"We were like":** Gooch, *Radiant*, 103.

57   **"sin as if":** See a related image at Deitch, Geiss, and Gruen, *Keith Haring*, 40–41.

58   **"a cutie"** and **"a great underplayed":** Gooch, *Radiant,* 130.

59   **"clones":** Keith stenciled "CLONES GO HOME" on the street at the entrance to the East Village. See an image of the stencil in Deitch, Geiss, and Gruen, *Keith Haring*, 58–59.

62   **"My parents have":** David Sheff, "Keith Haring: Just Say Know," *Rolling Stone*, August 10, 1989.

62   **"*Keeeeith!*"** and **"This is *not*":** Quoted by Craig Koller, in conversation with author, March 31, 2025.

5. HUMAN ON DOLPHIN, GRAFFITI

66 **"quite bizarre"** and **"More than anything":** John Gruen, *Keith Haring: The Authorized Biography* (New York: Fireside, 1991), 56.

67 **"I was drawing"** and **"Most of them":** Ed McCormack, "Pop Goes the Easel," *New York Daily News*, August 4, 1985.

67 **"*The public has*":** Keith Haring, *Keith Haring Journals* (New York: Viking, 1996), 13.

69 **"I was thinking":** *Notes from the Pop Underground*, edited by Peter Belsito (Berkeley: The Gasp of San Francisco, 1985), 100.

69 **"demanded to be":** Keith Haring, interview by Terri Gross, *Fresh Air*, September 3, 1987, WHYY, Philadelphia.

71 **"The first image,"** **"At the time,"** and **"In the beginning":** Belsito, *Notes from the Pop Underground*, 100.

72 **"Keith was mortified":** Ingrid Sischy, "Kid Haring," *Vanity Fair*, July 1997.

74 **"All of a sudden":** Gruen, *Keith Haring*, 61.

76 **"The panels were"** and **"It felt incredible":** Gruen, *Keith Haring*, 68.

78 **"What does it":** Jason Rubell, "Keith Haring: The Last Interview," *Arts Magazine*, September 1990.

79 **"That's your part"** and **"I only do":** Keith Haring, "Keith Haring," *Flash Art* 116 (March 1984): 22.

79 **"They'd go off":** ArtCenter College of Design, "Keith Haring: A Public Thing," video, posted June 26, 2023, https://www.youtube.com/watch?v=PStU7VWxIak.

80 **"domination, power, and":** Doris Whitbeck, "Graffiti Outgrowth," *Hartford Courant*, June 1, 1983.

80 **"babies represent the":** Robert Farris Thompson, "Requiem for the Degas of the B-Boys, Keith Haring," *Artforum*, no date [1990], accessed at https://www.artforum.com/features/requiem-for-the-degas-of-the-b-boys-keith-haring-204839/.

80 **"Sometimes the dog"** and **"either the location":** "Keith Haring Compilation, 1978–1985," KHA 0894, Keith Haring Archives, Keith Haring Foundation, New York, New York.

80 **"Millions of passengers":** August Mutzdorf, "Berlin Graffiti," *Time*, November 24, 1986.

81 **"Don't you have"** and **"really bored":** "Ten Commandments—Bordeaux Exhibition, La Realidad Inventada, Spanish TV," no date, KHA 0693, Keith Haring Archives.

81 **"So many people":** Keith Haring, "The Subway Is Still My Favorite Place to Draw," in *31 Subway Drawings* (Princeton: Princeton University Press; and New York: No More Rulers, 2021), 9. This essay is reprinted from Keith Haring, *Art in Transit* (New York: Harmony Books, 1984).

82 **"The worst thing":** "20/20 Segment by Dick Schaap," Spring 1986, transcript, Keith Haring files, Kutztown Area Historical Society, Kutztown, Pennsylvania.

82 **"I'm white":** Carey Lovelace, "Graffiti-ist Chalks Up Art Stardom," *Los Angeles Times*, May 13, 1984.

83 **"I think in," "The subway drawings," "Art was the,"** and **"And it was":** Rubell, "Keith Haring: The Last Interview," 1990.

SIDEBAR: WHAT DO THE IMAGES MEAN?

84 **"Keith Haring's picture-word," "sometimes functions as," "any person who,"** and **"stands for Walt":** Albertina, "Keith Haring. The Alphabet," no date [2018]. See also *Keith Haring*, ed. Dieter Buchart, Elsy Lahner, and Klaus Albert Schröder (Vienna: Albertina Museum, 2018).

SIDEBAR: ARE THE HUMAN FIGURES MALES?

85 **"No," "They don't have,"** and **"If they have":** Daniel Drenger, "Art and Life: An Interview with Keith Haring," *Columbia Art Review* (Spring 1988): 50.

6. DJ: MUSIC

88 **"I mean, he":** Jeffrey Deitch, Suzanne Geiss, and Julia Gruen, in cooperation with the Estate of Keith Haring, *Keith Haring* (New York: Rizzoli, 2014), 146.

88 **"It is Juan":** John Gruen, *Keith Haring: The Authorized Biography* (New York: Fireside, 1991), 77.

90 **"I work surrounded," "Music in New,"** and **"And for me":** *Keith Haring a Milano*, edited by Alessandro Galasso (Milan: Johan & Levi, 2008), quoted in Sotheby's, "Keith Haring's

Dazzling Ode to the Music That Inspired Him," February 12, 2023, accessed at https://www.sothebys.com/en/articles/keith-harings-dazzling-ode-to-the-music-that-inspired-him.

92 **"To me music":** Clare Ann Matz, "Keith Haring Interviewed by Clare Ann Matz, Pisa, Italy, 1988—TuttoMondo (All Over the World) Mural," video, posted April 29, 2021, https://www.youtube.com/watch?v=yDYykA8WVqw.

92 **"a great saxophonist"** and **"He had this":** Hillary Moss, "Decoding Keith Haring's Early Works," *New York Times Style Magazine*, November 5, 2015.

94 **"Everyone was there":** "Paradise Garage: The Oral History of NYC's Greatest Club," *TimeOut*, August 21, 2018.

94 **"He moved in," "It was definitely," "But it was,"** and **"Keith felt acceptance":** Benny Soto, in conversation with author, April 8, 2025.

96 **"One day Futura"** and **"We had no":** The Keith Haring Foundation, "Conversations," January 1997, accessed at https://www.haring.com/!/selected_writing/conversations.

97 **"Breakdancing was a"** and **"So my drawings":** Gruen, *Keith Haring*, 90.

99 **"I guess I":** "Interview with Broad Street Studio," no date, KH 0794, Keith Haring Archives, Keith Haring Foundation, New York, New York.

102 **"The whole experience":** Gruen, *Keith Haring*, 89. For a similar perspective, see Gay Men's Health Crisis, "Keep on Dancin': A Dance Party Celebrating the Spirit of the Paradise Garage," July 31, 2024, accessed at https://www.gmhc.org/keep-on-dancin-a-dance-party-celebrating-the-spirit-of-the-paradise-garage/.

102 **"losing a lover":** Keith Haring, *Keith Haring Journals* (New York: Viking, 1996), 173.

7. AGAINST NUKES: PROTEST

106 **"No nukes!"** and **"I Hate Nuclear":** Paul L. Montgomery, "Throngs Fill Manhattan to Protest Nuclear Weapons," *New York Times*, June 13, 1982.

109 **"We're thinking of"** and **"There are no":** Robin Herman, "Rally Speakers Decry Cost of Nuclear Weapons," *New York Times*, June 13, 1982.

111 **"Another drawing today," "He has a,"** and **"I guess it":** Cliff Fyman, "Interview with Keith Haring," September 26, 1984; quoted in Brad Gooch, *Radiant: The Life and Line of Keith Haring* (New York: Harper, 2024), 251–252.

112 **"Some people were"** and **"It's fun when":** Vince Aletti, "An Interview with Keith Haring," *Keith Haring: Future Primeval*, ed. Barry Blinderman (New York: Abbeville Press, 1990), 97, 100.

114 **"They had binoculars"** and **"I tell you":** Guy D. Garcia, "People," *Time*, November 3, 1986.

115 **"The human chain":** Frieder Reimold, "Wall Attracts Interest in Berlin," Associated Press article, October 30, 1986.

115 **"It's for people":** "Keith Haring Paints Mural on Berlin Wall," *New York Times*, October 24, 1986.

115 **"a political and":** "Off-the-Wall Berlin Art," United Press International article, October 26, 1986.

116 **"For me the Berlin"** and **"It is a metaphor":** Reimold, "Wall Attracts Interest in Berlin," October 30, 1986.

116 **"It is impossible," "There was one," "In one picture,"** and **"It was not":** Keith Haring, *Keith Haring Journals* (New York: Viking, 1996), 221.

117 **"While there I":** Haring, *Keith Haring Journals*, 222.

SIDEBAR: WORLD PEACE

119 **"harmony," "unity,"** and **"the world at":** "Interferenze Videoproduzioni Via S. Martino, 59-56100 Pisa, Italia—Videoritratti Di Keith Haring," no date [June 1989], transcript, Keith Haring files, Kutztown Area Historical Society, Kutztown, Pennsylvania.

8. MICHAEL STEWART—USA FOR AFRICA: RACE AND RETRIBUTION

122 **"The whole downtown":** Brad Gooch, *Radiant: The Life and Line of Keith Haring* (New York: Harper, 2024), 215.

122 **"Madonna Loves Keith":** Natasha Gural, "Keith Haring's Refrigerator Door, Andy Warhol's Moose Head, and Christo's Plan for 'The Gates' Flesh Out Wonderfully Weird Sale," *Forbes*, April 28, 2021.

125 **"He was completely"** and **"It was like":** Gooch, *Radiant*, 218.

126 **"the unfortunate death":** Sam Roberts, "Death Stirs Police Brutality Charges," *New York Times*, September 29, 1983.

126　**"Keith was ranting":** *The Andy Warhol Diaries*, edited by Pat Hackett (New York: Twelve, 1989), 542.

127　**"It could have":** Erik Nielsen, "'It Could Have Been Me,'" National Public Radio (NPR), September 16, 2013, accessed at https://www.npr.org/sections/codeswitch/2013/09/16/221821224/it-could-have-been-me-the-1983-death-of-a-nyc-graffiti-artist.

127　**"I hired his"** and **"I went to":** Matt Barker, "The Brutal Death That Politicized New York's Art World," British Broadcasting Company (BBC), July 15, 2019, accessed at https://www.bbc.com/culture/article/20190710-the-brutal-death-that-politicised-new-yorks-art-world.

129　**"Today I read":** Keith Haring, *Keith Haring Journals* (New York: Viking, 1996), 124–125.

129　**"Yes, to a degree":** Daniel Drenger, "Art and Life: An Interview with Keith Haring," *Columbia Art Review* (Spring 1988): 49.

132　**"Most white men," "All stories of,"** and **"I'm sure inside":** Haring, *Keith Haring Journals*, 124.

133　**"Maybe I was black":** Drenger, "Art and Life," 51.

133　**"I'm terrifically comfortable"** and **"But then":** John Gruen, *Keith Haring: The Authorized Biography* (New York: Fireside, 1991), 88.

134　**"I look at":** Gruen, *Keith Haring*, 139.

134　**"I was familiar"** and **"'Cause I thought":** Arnaldo Cruz-Malavé, *Queer Latino* Testimonio, *Keith Haring, and Juanito Xtravaganza: Hard Tails* (New York: Palgrave Macmillan, 2007), 41.

134　**"When I saw":** Gruen, *Keith Haring*, 141.

134　**"I cooked and":** Gruen, *Keith Haring*, 140.

136　**"I knew that"** and **"He'd make it":** Cruz-Malavé, *Queer Latino* Testimonio, 40.

SIDEBAR: WAS KEITH RACIST?

137　**"He's really trying"** and **"Keith says that":** Quoted in Tim Murphy, "A New Book Explores the Racial Politics of Iconic Artist Keith Haring," *TheBody.com*, October 6, 2020. See also Ricardo Montez, *Keith Haring's Line* (Durham: Duke University Press, 2020).

9. ANDY MOUSE: MONEY AND FAME

140 **"These drawings had," "Word had gotten," "an art statement,"** and **"we didn't want":** John Gruen, *Keith Haring: The Authorized Biography* (New York: Fireside, 1991), 148.

143 **"If commercialism is":** Edward Hill, "'Fast Food' Artist Makes Big Bucks," Associated Press article, June 1, 1986.

143 **"Capitalist":** Michael Gross, "Notes on Fashion," *New York Times*, April 22, 1986.

143 **"Ultimately, I don't"** and **"I'm more interested":** Janet S. Tyson, "Artist Stays One Step Ahead of Chic," *Peninsula Times-Tribune* (Palo Alto, California), December 11, 1985.

144 **"I wanna be":** Paula Span, "Subways to Museums: Graffiti's Scrawl of Success," *Washington Post*, December 29, 1985.

144 **"there's not really":** "Weekend NY: Keith Haring," April 27, 1988, video, KH 0672, Keith Haring Archives, Keith Haring Foundation, New York, New York.

146 **"He gave me"** and **"I didn't know":** Brad Gooch, *Radiant: The Life and Line of Keith Haring* (New York: Harper, 2024), 204.

147 **"They were so":** *The Andy Warhol Diaries*, edited by Pat Hackett (New York: Twelve, 1989), 530.

148 **"I don't know"** and **"Obviously, it was":** Gruen, *Keith Haring*, 92.

150 **"Of course, it's"** and **"It's so transparent":** Gruen, *Keith Haring*, 93.

150 **"Keith just wanted," "And he wanted," "Keith wanted to,"** and **"So we got":** Hackett, *The Andy Warhol Diaries*, 688.

151 **"Keith Haring's work," "But there never," "fast food," "It's a good,"** and **"It's boogeying on":** Edward Hill, "Keith Haring Takes Modern Art to the Masses," Associated Press article, May 9, 1986.

152 **"who correctly point":** Suzanne Muchnic, "The Galleries: La Cienega Area," *Los Angeles Times*, June 10, 1988.

152 **"Keith Haring isn't"** and **"And they have":** Hackett, *The Andy Warhol Diaries*, 585.

152 **"the most important"** and **"The museum and":** Keith Haring, *Keith Haring Journals* (New York: Viking, 1996), 117.

153 **"It's really funny," "They want to," "I should be," "pure art," "The only time,"** and **"When I do":** Haring, *Keith Haring Journals*, 175–176.

10. DANCING FEMALES: CHILDREN

158 **"The students have," "By the time," "Don't be upset," "You don't exactly," "They don't seem,"** and **"This experience is":** Cynthia Benjamin, "Graffiti Artist Opens New Vistas for Iowa Schoolchildren," Associated Press article, June 10, 1984.

160 **"I would love," "Children are the,"** and **"Children are color-blind":** Keith Haring, *Keith Haring Journals* (New York: Viking, 1996), 98.

161 **"hardest audience":** Kanchalee Svetvilas, "Art on the Go," *Iowa City Press-Citizen*, May 23, 1989.

161 **"I was totally":** John Gruen, *Keith Haring: The Authorized Biography* (New York: Fireside, 1991), 113.

162 **"I don't think"** and **"I really like":** "Keith Haring: Interview by John Romine, *Upstart* (1983); quoted in Brad Gooch, *Radiant: The Life and Line of Keith Haring* (New York: Harper, 2024), 234.

163 **"a little baby":** Keith Haring, *Keith Haring Journals* (New York: Viking, 1996), 185.

165 **"I sang Madison"** and **"The feeling of":** Haring, *Keith Haring Journals*, 241–242.

165 **"He loved doing"** and **"If there was":** Gooch, *Radiant*, 29.

165 **"The reason that":** Haring, *Keith Haring Journals*, 98.

166 **"Happy birthday to":** "Happy Birthday to Keith from Ernst Horn Elementary," no date [1989], KHA 0579, Keith Haring Archives, Keith Haring Foundation, New York, New York.

166 **"It was the"** and **"A book full":** Svetvilas, "Art on the Go."

166 **"It's probably from"** and **"And kids can":** Gruen, *Keith Haring*, 114.

167 **"*I love life*," "I appreciate everything," "It is this,"** and **"Maybe you don't":** Haring, *Keith Haring Journals*, 123.

168 **"I can tell":** "Off the Wall with Keith and the Kids," video, WTTW, Chicago, 2018, accessed at https://www.pbs.org/video/off-the-wall-with-keith-and-the-kids-1tjcuz/.

168 **"He's eating the"** and **"It puts [the children]":** Joanne Furio, "Hospital Promotes the Art of Healing," *Newsday* (New York, New York), January 8, 1990.

170 **"I think there's"** and **"It's definitely helpful":** Gooch, *Radiant*, 341.

171 **"Whatever else I":** Haring, *Keith Haring Journals*, 180.

SIDEBAR: LA II—TEENAGE GRAFFITI KING

172 **"It stood out":** Gruen, *Keith Haring*, 80.

172 **"Yo, why you":** Gooch, *Radiant*, 177.

172 **"You *know* LA II," "Yeah, it's me!"** and **"Prove to me":** Gruen, *Keith Haring*, 80.

173 **"Little Angel," "I put the,"** and **"So LA II":** Gruen, *Keith Haring*, 81.

173 **"My relationship with":** Richard Whiddington, "Street Artist and Keith Haring Collaborator Angel Ortiz's New Graffiti-Inspired Works Bottle the Vibe of 1980s New York," *Artnet*, May 22, 2023, accessed at https://news.artnet.com/art-world/angel-ortiz-ode-2-nyc-show-keith-haring-2306998.

11. CRACK IS WACK: DRUGS

177 **"Keith could get," "I was really,"** and **"I was from":** Benny Soto, in conversation with author, April 8, 2025.

178 **"Crack makes you":** David Sheff, "Keith Haring: Just Say Know," *Rolling Stone*, August 10, 1989.

179 **"I think you're,"** *Holy shit*, and ***Am I an*:** Soto, interview, April 8, 2025.

179 **"really distressing because":** Jeffrey Deitch, Suzanne Geiss, and Julia Gruen, in cooperation with the Estate of Keith Haring, *Keith Haring* (New York: Rizzoli, 2014), 390.

179 **"We called these":** Deitch, Geiss, Gruen, and the Estate of Keith Haring, *Keith Haring*, 390.

179 **"I felt like":** Soto, interview, April 8, 2025.

179 **"We proceeded to":** Deitch, Geiss, Gruen, and the Estate of Keith Haring, *Keith Haring*, 390.

180 **"just say no":** Ronald Reagan, "Address to the Nation on the Campaign Against Drug Abuse," September 14, 1986, accessed at https://www.reaganlibrary.gov/archives/speech/address-nation-campaign-against-drug-abuse.

180 **"Inspired by Benny":** Deitch, Geiss, Gruen, and the Estate of Keith Haring, *Keith Haring*, 390.

181 **"CRACK IS WACK":** See image at Deitch, Geiss, Gruen, and the Estate of Keith Haring, *Keith Haring*, 393.

182 **"During the day"** and **"Cars went past":** Deitch, Geiss, Gruen, and the Estate of Keith Haring, *Keith Haring*, 391.

183 **"The thing that":** *Drawing the Line: A Portrait of Keith Haring*, directed and produced by Elizabeth Aubert Schlumberger, 1989.

183 **"Every time the"** and **"NBC did a":** Deitch, Geiss, Gruen, and the Estate of Keith Haring, *Keith Haring*, 391.

183 **"The sentiment is"** and **"Supposedly, Reagan is":** Lisa Faye Kaplan, "Not-So-Hot Spot Opens in Manhattan," *Citizen Register* (Ossining, New York), September 18, 1986.

184 **"I was relieved":** Marvine Howe and Frank J. Prial, "New York Day by Day," *New York Times*, September 19, 1986.

184 **"Crack Is It":** Howe and Prial, "New York Day by Day."

184 **"probably crack users":** Deitch, Geiss, Gruen, and the Estate of Keith Haring, *Keith Haring*, 392.

185 **"We picked him"** and **"We shook him":** Phoebe Hoban, *Basquiat: A Quick Killing in Art* (New York: Viking, 1998), 2.

186 **"That's Jean-Michel":** Brad Gooch, *Radiant: The Life and Line of Keith Haring* (New York: Harper, 2024), 370.

188 **"It's only as":** Deitch, Geiss, Gruen, and the Estate of Keith Haring, *Keith Haring*, 455.

SIDEBAR: A GIFT FROM KEITH

189 **"After I got"** and **"After all, I":** Soto, interview, April 8, 2025.

189 **"I love you":** Benny Soto, text message to author, April 9, 2025.

189 **"I was blown"** and **"I wanted him":** Soto, interview, April 8, 2025.

12. STOP AIDS: HIV

193   **"I was major"** and **"If I didn't":** David Sheff, "Keith Haring: Just Say Know," *Rolling Stone*, August 10, 1989.

193   **"I immediately got":** John Gruen, *Keith Haring: The Authorized Biography* (New York: Fireside, 1991), 187.

194   **"I went over"** and **"You realize that":** Jeffrey Deitch, Suzanne Geiss, and Julia Gruen, in cooperation with the Estate of Keith Haring, *Keith Haring* (New York: Rizzoli, 2014), 444.

196   **"Because of the"** and **"So the more":** Gruen, *Keith Haring*, 189.

197   **"I knew the baby," "I knew the dog," "And I am,"** and **"And [Keith] was":** Andrea-Jo Wilson, "From Friendship to Foundation," *Foyer*, November 30, 2023.

197   **"incredibly beautiful," "smart, sympathetic, and clever,"** and **"a friendship *not*":** Gruen, *Keith Haring*, 188.

198   **"incredibly compassionate":** Gruen, *Keith Haring*, 189.

198   **"All I know":** Keith Haring, *Keith Haring Journals* (New York: Viking, 1996), 231.

198   **"When I leave"** and **"At the door":** Gruen, *Keith Haring*, 195.

198   **"I remember Keith":** Brad Gooch, *Radiant: The Life and Line of Keith Haring* (New York: Harper, 2024), 383.

199   **"*Todos Juntos Podemos*":** See images at "Keith Haring's Barcelona Mural: A Vibrant Call to Action," *Public Delivery*, September 25, 2024, accessed at https://publicdelivery.org/keith-haring-barcelona/.

199   **"an attempt to"** and **"The message was":** Haring, *Keith Haring Journals*, 245.

201   **"I think it's":** "Silence = Death," directed and produced by Rosa von Praunheim, 1990, accessed at https://www.youtube.com/watch?v=dgKgPFl7960&t=2708s.

201   **"Debbie Dick"** and **"Wear Rubbers!":** See image at Ana Flores, "Keith Haring: Exponente Gay del Arte Urbano Vivió con VIH," *Homosensual*, May 4, 2022, accessed at https://www.homosensual.com/cultura/arte/keith-haring-exponente-gay-del-arte-urbano-vivio-con-vih/.

202   **"Peter, I really"** and **"Can you stop":** *Keith Haring: Street Art Boy*, directed by Ben Anthony, produced by Ben Anthony, Michael Kantor, Janet Lee, and Alice Rhodes, 2020.

202 **"Sure," "The studio was," "And there was,"** and **"And I very":** Peter Staley, in conversation with author, March 28, 2025.

203 **"Act up! Fight back!":** "200 Arrested in AIDS Protest," United Press International article, March 29, 1989.

204 **"10,000 New York":** See image at Deitch, Geiss, Gruen, and the Estate of Keith Haring, *Keith Haring*, 445.

206 **"I have so":** Sheff, "Keith Haring," August 10, 1989.

207 **"I really want"** and **"I think I":** Haring, *Keith Haring Journals*, 270.

207 **"The hardest thing"** and **"I'm so scared":** Sheff, "Keith Haring," August 10, 1989.

208 **"He was just," "When he tried," "There were now,"** and **"He just didn't":** Gruen, *Keith Haring*, 218.

208 **"He was really," "You could see,"** and **"Finally, he drew":** Gooch, *Radiant*, 416.

EPILOGUE: REBELLIOUS

210 **"screamed with dire":** Andrew Yarrow, "Friends Memorialize Keith Haring in Song and Playful Reminiscence," *New York Times*, May 5, 1990.

210 **"RESIST!":** Keith Haring Foundation, "RESIST!" June 2, 2020, accessed at https://foundationblog.haring.com/topics/activism.

211 **"I learned a lot":** John Gruen, *Keith Haring: The Authorized Biography* (New York: Fireside, 1991), 220–221.

213 **"best go-go"** and **"And the winner":** Yarrow, "Friends Memorialize Keith Haring in Song and Playful Reminiscence," May 5, 1990. Ellipses added after "And the winner is."

213 **"There may never":** Holland Cotter, "Dancing Again with Keith Haring, Day-Glo Populist," *New York Times*, June 27, 1997.

214 **"on the street":** Max Lakin, "Keith Haring's Legacy Is Not Found at the Museum," *New York Times*, April 18, 2024. I am indebted to Lakin for this point.

IMAGE CREDITS

89	© Laura Levine/Getty Images
91	Photo by Tseng Kwong Chi © Muna Tseng Dance Projects, Inc. Art @ Keith Haring Foundation
94	© Tina Paul; Artwork ©Keith Haring Foundation
97	© Martha Cooper
98	Photo by Tseng Kwong Chi © Muna Tseng Dance Projects, Inc. Art @ Keith Haring Foundation
101	Photo by Tseng Kwong Chi © Muna Tseng Dance Projects, Inc. Art @ Keith Haring Foundation
105	© Keith Haring Foundation
107	© Joseph Szkodzinski; Artwork ©Keith Haring Foundation
108	© Keith Haring Foundation
111	Photo by Tseng Kwong Chi © Muna Tseng Dance Projects, Inc. Art @ Keith Haring Foundation
114	© Patrick Piel/Getty Images; Artwork ©Keith Haring Foundation
119	Photo by Tseng Kwong Chi © Muna Tseng Dance Projects, Inc. Art @ Keith Haring Foundation
121	© Keith Haring Foundation
123	Courtesy Guernsey's, New York
126	© Ben Buchanan. All rights reserved 2025 / Bridgeman Images
131	© Keith Haring Foundation
132	Photo by Tseng Kwong Chi © Muna Tseng Dance Projects, Inc. Art @ Keith Haring Foundation
135	Photographic reproduction from Andy Warhol's 35mm negative. Keith Haring and Juan Rivera. 1986. @ 2025 The Andy Warhol Foundation for the Visual Arts, Inc./Licensed by Artists Rights Society [ARS], New York
139	© Keith Haring Foundation
141	Courtesy of Michael G. Long/Artwork ©Keith Haring Foundation
142	Photo by Tseng Kwong Chi © Muna Tseng Dance Projects, Inc. Art @ Keith Haring Foundation
145	© Patrick McMullen/Getty Images
148	Photo by Tseng Kwong Chi © Muna Tseng Dance Projects, Inc. Art @ Keith Haring Foundation
154	Paulo Fridman/Corbis via Getty Images
157	© Keith Haring Foundation
159	© Rodney White; Artwork ©Keith Haring Foundation
162	Photo by Allen Haring. Courtesy of the Haring Family.
163	Photo by Allen Haring. Courtesy of the Haring family.
164	© Keith Haring Foundation
167	© Timothy Schoon; Artwork ©Keith Haring Foundation
169	© Keith Haring Foundation

Index

Page numbers in *italic* refer to illustrations.